I0536258

"In her book, *Our Road to Emmaus,* Brenda Troutman shares her story of living with a burden of shame, even after she accepted Jesus as her Savior. God had forgiven her, yes, but she couldn't forgive herself. She likens her journey to complete redemption—accepting the act that resulted in a decades-long burden of shame as part of her testimony—to the journey the two disciples took on that first Easter as they questioned the events that had taken place that morning.

"It was more than a seven-mile walk from Jerusalem to Emmaus. It was a spiritual journey as well, as the Lord Himself joined them and gently cleared their confusion. Aren't we all on a journey that takes us down a road riddled with potholes of confusion and doubt? But the journey we take is one of growth, whether or not we see it as such. If you're going through a time of heartbreak or grief, or if you simply want to see Jesus more clearly in your life, Brenda's testimony is sure to give you hope and strength for the next step."

—*Michele Huey, Author & Speaker*

Our Road to Emmaus

Walking with Jesus
through Difficult Times

Brenda Troutman

RIVER BIRCH PRESS

Daphne, Alabama

Our Road to Emmaus by Brenda Troutman
Copyright ©2022 Brenda Troutman
All rights reserved. This book is protected under the copyright laws of the United States of America. This book may not be copied or reprinted for commercial gain or profit.

Scripture quotations marked NIV are taken from THE HOLY BIBLE: New International Version ©1978 by the New York International Bible Society, used by permission of Zondervan Bible Publishers.

ISBN 978-1-956365-33-7 (print)
ISBN 978-1-956365-34-4 (e-book)

For Worldwide Distribution
Printed in the USA.

River Birch Press
P.O. Box 868, Daphne, AL 36526

CONTENTS

This book is dedicated to Connie Cope, my beautiful sister in Christ. God brought her into my story at a time when I needed her the most, and I am forever grateful for her obedience to come and minister to me.

PREFACE

Everyone faces difficult times in their lives. When these times come, we often have difficulty grasping where Jesus could be in the middle of the struggle. Through this book, I desire for you to see that Jesus always walks with us. He is right there through good times and bad, upholding us and giving us guidance. This journey of life can lead us down roads we don't want to be on, but the struggle is always for a purpose: to draw us closer to our Savior.

I have been on this journey myself. I have walked a road of staying in my own guilt and shame, afraid to allow Jesus to change me. I was a believer, but I wasn't living the abundant life that Jesus promised to those who trust Him. My struggle was shame and embarrassment, even after I knew I had been forgiven. Through it all, Jesus was right beside me. I couldn't always see Him because often all I could see was my shame.

Then the moment came when I saw Jesus clearly and realized that He had taken that shame away on the cross. I'll unfold my story of redemption as we journey on this road together. I hope that through my struggle, you will see that Jesus can take your life and make it more beautiful than ever. And I hope you will be encouraged to share your story of adversity and triumph.

Perhaps you are finding yourself on the same type of road. Maybe your path has taken a turn you were not expecting, or you hit a bump in the road you never saw coming. Taking a walk through this book is a great place to begin the redemptive process. Jesus will meet you along your path if you allow Him.

Your road might be smooth right now, you don't have any significant problems, and you don't think you need this journey. Remember, though, that Jesus warned us in John 16:33 that we will have trouble in this world. Preparing for anything life could throw your way is always a good idea. Read this book now so that when problems come, you are rooted deeply in Christ. You will find the struggle so much easier when He takes the burden.

At the end of each chapter, you will be encouraged to write your thoughts and prayers. Have a notebook or journal handy, so you can put words to what Jesus is speaking to your heart on each step of the road. Focus questions and Scripture passages are also available to help you think deeper and grow your relationship with Christ.

I encourage you to find a small group with whom you can share what you've learned on your journey. Most of all, allow yourself to be immersed in the love of Christ as He walks along side you.

ACKNOWLEDGMENTS

I would first like to thank my Lord and Savior Jesus Christ, without whom I can do nothing but with whom I can do all things. It is only by His will and grace that this book exists.

Thank you to my husband, Chris, who supports my endeavors to try new things and is there to help me be as successful as possible.

Thank you to Michele Huey, who guided me through the publishing process and was such a support and encouragement every step of the way.

Thank you to Teri Gray, my prayer warrior and biggest supporter. She has been my greatest encourager from the very beginning of this project and continues to support and pray for me through everything.

INTRODUCTION

I am always amazed when a passage of Scripture becomes so personal that I can't let it go. One passage the Lord keeps bringing to my mind is Luke 24:13-35. Here we are told about two men walking from Jerusalem to a town about seven miles away called Emmaus. Downcast, they discussed the events they had witnessed surrounding Jesus' crucifixion.

Another person came alongside them, but they did not recognize Him as Jesus. However, once they listened to Him recount the Scriptures that spoke of the Messiah and then sat down with Him to break bread, their eyes were opened, and Jesus disappeared. They knew they had encountered the living Christ. So great was their joy that they immediately rushed back to Jerusalem, found the disciples, and told them this wonderful thing that had happened to them.

Lately, I am urged to think about my road to Emmaus when this passage comes to mind. We are all on a journey like the one these two people experienced. As we walk this road of life, Jesus is always there, ready to teach us and help us understand, but we often do not recognize Him. We struggle, allow our faces to be downcast, and mourn over how we think things should have turned out. However, when we open our eyes and see His presence, we stand amazed at what Jesus can do and have the incredible opportunity to tell others about it.

These two men's accounts are especially relevant when traveling a road filled with difficulties or pain. The two men on the road to Emmaus had believed Jesus had come to rescue Israel, but perhaps they had been wrong. Jesus had been crucified, and they had trouble figuring it out. They were mourning the loss of the One they thought would redeem Israel and were afraid for the future. Life hadn't turned out the way they imagined it, and they just couldn't understand why. Then in walked Jesus, and what a spectacular journey He took them on! He can take us on the same walk if we let Him.

Take some time to read your way through Luke 24:13-35. Allow yourself to think about your own road to Emmaus. Walk with the men through downcast faces, times of struggling, and life not turning out the way they thought it would. Join them as they invite Jesus in and find redemption as you break bread with them. Put your own journey in the context of what these men went through and allow Jesus onto your path.

As you walk down this road, take the time at the end of each chapter to answer the questions provided, meditate on the passages of Scripture, and write about what you have learned or are processing. Writing out your thoughts and feelings is an great way to interpret everything you are picking up or going through on your journey. Journaling allows you to take what is happening with your thoughts and emotions and release them into the Lord's hands. In the future, you can look back on these journal entries and remember everything the Lord brought you through. If you are new to journaling, it may be difficult at first, but it is worth it; give it a try and see what God can show you!

Now step out with me on the road to Emmaus, and let's journey together.

1

The Journey

Now that same day two of them were going to a village called Emmaus, about seven miles from Jerusalem (Luke 24:13).

We hear it all the time: life is a journey. In the case of the two men on the road to Emmaus, the journey was about seven miles. If they walked at a leisurely pace, this trip would probably have taken about three hours. Portions of the journey on that dusty road would have been more challenging to navigate than others.

Near the end of the road, fatigue would probably have set in. A lot can occur in three hours and seven miles, and as we walk with them on our journey, we will see that a lot happened to these men. But first, let us start right where they began—with the first step.

Let's remember why they were on this journey in the first place. They had just witnessed the horrifying death of the One they thought would save Israel from Roman rule. The man who had brought them joy and hope had suddenly and horribly been taken from them. All their hopes and dreams had been ripped out from under them.

Now what? With their dreams smashed, they wondered what life would look like from then on out. Should they forget about Jesus and return to life as it was before? Everything they hoped for while Jesus was alive had now been lost. They had no idea what the future might hold and were afraid of what would come. Their lives had been turned upside down.

Now think about your life. So much happens to us and around us every day. Picture yourself on a dusty road like the men in this passage of Scripture. Consider the events in your life that have changed you. Remember the things that have left you confused and unsure. Think about any difficulties you are experiencing as you read these pages. Is the uncertainty of the future weighing on you? Are you wondering and worried about what might be coming next? Are you discouraged because life hasn't turned out like you thought it would? Have events outside of your control turned your world upside down? If so, you're not alone. This is where so many people find themselves today, and it's exactly where the men on the road to Emmaus found themselves.

My Journey

I can relate to being on a road like the one described above. In 1998, when I had one semester left to finish my college career, all I had to do was fulfill my student teaching assignment. That's when I discovered I was pregnant. This wasn't just bad timing; I wasn't married. That may not seem like a big deal in today's world where it seems to be the norm, but at that time and in my small town, it was the one sin you couldn't hide, a stain on your reputation that no one would forget.

At the time, I wasn't following the Lord, but I had grown up in church, believing in God and knowing right from wrong. I had accepted Jesus as my Savior when I was twelve at Vacation Bible School, but I had turned to my own way. I knew this would frustrate my family, and I had no idea how my pregnancy would affect my future. Would I finish college? Could I possibly still follow my dream of becoming a teacher? How could I face the disappointment of the people I loved?

This part of the story worked out. I dropped out of college for a year but eventually finished my degree. At first, I worked as a substitute teacher and ultimately became a full-time teacher. In 2000, when my son was eighteen months old, I married his father, and we are still married twenty-two years later.

My real battle came when I decided I wanted to return to the Lord. When my son was about two, I tried a few churches to find my niche. In the first church I visited, I heard a couple of ladies talking about me in another room, calling me "the girl who had that baby before she was married." I went home discouraged, feeling like a failure. How could God ever forgive me? I was so ashamed and insecure.

To even consider attending church again took me a long time. But when my son was five and my second child was two, I decided to try another church. Surely, if they didn't know the timing of my son's birth, I could start fresh. Nobody talked about me there; in fact, nobody talked to me at all. I left and didn't go back.

Finally, in 2004, I found the perfect church home where I still attend today. The people in this church very quickly became my family in Christ. They loved and accepted me. Due to my shame, however, I didn't tell anyone that my first child was born out of wedlock. When my wedding anniversary would come around, I wouldn't tell anyone because I was terrified of the question, "How many years have you been married?" They just had to do the math to figure it out, and I wasn't going to let that happen. This was the beginning of a long road that I stumbled down until I found the beautiful redemption the Lord had for me.

The Different Roads of Life

Wherever you are on your own road to Emmaus, remember that God always has a purpose. He is always at work on your behalf. Most of the time, what we think should have happened in life didn't. The plans we had were not necessarily God's will for us. We walk down the dusty road confused, wondering what to do next. But God is never confused. In fact, He knows exactly what He is doing, and when we are found in Him, His purposes are always for our good (Romans 8:28).

God has a road map that He perfectly weaves together for all our lives, but we can only see the little dot on that map where we struggle today. What we may see now are the dusty road and the potholes. It's hard to get our eyes off the problems and onto Jesus. There is a place for us in the big picture, but we can't see it yet. So, like the men on the road to Emmaus, we walk on, trying to figure everything out on our own.

Sometimes, this life journey gets rough; we run into deep potholes that we never anticipated. Sometimes, it seems like we're cruising along freshly paved roads. We need to take our focus off the condition of the road and remember the One who constructed the road. God is the master builder who puts the road in place and lays it out perfectly.

The potholes are no accident but teach us how to depend on His guidance to drive through and around them. Sometimes this road of life will lead us around a blind curve into a big and unexpected pothole that shakes our entire world. However, God knew we would hit that pothole before it happened. Don't be afraid. He can also send a tow truck to pull us out of the ditch. Psalm 40:2 reads, "He lifted me out of the slimy pit, out of the mud and mire; he set my feet on a rock and gave me a firm place to stand." Even when the road seems too hard, remember that God still built it, and He knows how to navigate you through those rough spots.

The freshly paved roads are there to give us rest when we need it most. We all long for life to be smooth like those newly paved roads. God gives us refreshing—peaceful times when we can rest in Him and soak in His goodness. Don't be tempted to put yourself on cruise control during those times. These smooth roads offer us an opportunity to gain experience as well. Don't be fooled into thinking you can't veer off into a ditch because the road is smooth. Enjoy those restoration times in the Lord's presence, and take the opportunity to learn from Him.

Sometimes there are hills to climb and valleys to pass through as we walk along the road of life. Sometimes we dig our own potholes; we create bumps in the road that God didn't design. He knows about and can use those difficulties too. And all the while, we have guardrails and road signs in His Word to steer us the right way. His Word gives us the bigger picture, plus we have other believers who guide us in the right direction. Praise and worship music can make the journey more joyful and peaceful.

God's Perfect Purpose

Never underestimate the power and presence of God in your journey, especially in times of confusion and doubt. When you don't understand, it is because God is doing something you cannot see. He has a bigger and better purpose for you than you could ever imagine, and He is working out His will for you and the entire world. Your journey is part of a tapestry that the God of all creation laid out before the beginning of time. Just think, everyone is on a road of their own, walking a journey different from everybody else's. Yet all those roads work together as a highway system, overlapping and sometimes converging into one master plan God laid out before He even created us. How exciting that you get to be a part of that!

We can see an obvious example of God having a bigger purpose in the life of Joseph. In Genesis 37, Joseph's brothers took his robe, threw him in a cistern, and sold him to the Ishmaelites. I can imagine that Joseph was confused on his journey to Egypt. Why would God allow such a terrible thing to happen? I'm sure that after having dreams of his brothers bowing down to him, this is not how he thought things would turn out.

Joseph was probably thinking, *If only I would have kept my mouth shut about those dreams, maybe things would be different.* This was quite a long trip with plenty of time to ponder these questions and think about regrets and what he could have done differently. Joseph found himself on a journey he couldn't possibly understand. He had no idea at the time that God was at work, allowing a terrible time in his life to secure the rescue of an entire nation.

Genesis 39 says when Joseph arrived in Egypt, he lived in the house of Potiphar, one of Pharaoh's officials. Because Joseph chose to be a man of integrity and remain faithful to the Lord, even in times of uncertainty, God blessed him. Joseph was put in charge of all Potiphar owned. His circumstances were looking up, and the road was becoming smooth again.

Then, Joseph hit a giant pothole. Potiphar's wife unjustly accused him of sexual assault, and Joseph was sent to prison, although he had done nothing wrong. How could God allow this? Joseph was so faithful. Why would God bring this kind of suffering? Again, God had a bigger purpose, a plan that did not just mean good things for Joseph but the salvation of an entire nation.

While Joseph sat in prison, Scripture tells us in Genesis 40 that Pharaoh became angry with his cupbearer and baker and threw them in jail. Because Joseph remained faithful, even after being unjustly imprisoned, the prison guard put him in charge of other prisoners. Consequently, the cupbearer and baker were landed under Joseph's watch. Later, when these two men had dreams, Joseph could interpret them.

When these two servants were released from prison, Joseph asked them to remember him before Pharaoh. He thought the tide had turned in his favor. Surely these men would tell Pharaoh about him, and he would be set free. But they did not. The baker was executed, just as his dream foretold, and the cupbearer was restored to his position but forgot about Joseph.

Joseph would remain captive for another two years before Pharaoh had a dream. In his dream, he was standing by the Nile, and out of the river came seven fat cows. The seven lean cows came out of the river and ate the seven fat cows. Pharaoh's second dream had a similar theme, as seven full heads of grain swallowed seven thin ones. Then the cupbearer suddenly remembered Joseph and his ability to interpret dreams, and he was asked to do so. Joseph explained the fat cows and grain represented seven good years of crops, followed by seven years of famine that the lean cows and thin grain portrayed.

Even though Joseph was able to interpret Pharaoh's dream, nothing had changed for him yet, or so he thought. How could God allow him to remain a slave? Consider this: if Joseph's brothers had not sold him into slavery, if Potiphar's wife had not accused him of assault, if the cupbearer had remembered to tell Pharaoh about him sooner, then the timing would not have been right for Joseph to interpret Pharaoh's dream. He wouldn't have made a plan to survive the upcoming famine, and the nation of Egypt and the surrounding areas wouldn't have been saved.

And the timing would have been off for him to be reconciled with his family. If just one of those terrible things hadn't happened, God's plan for saving many people would not have come to pass. As each event unfolded in Joseph's life, it must have seemed hopeless to him at the moment. However, each event was significant in the big picture that couldn't be seen at the time.

Now, look at Jesus' journey. Here was the Creator of the universe, the King of all creation. He came to save the lost, to give us an eternity with Him. Jesus came to Earth through a miraculous yet humble birth, showed His power with many miracles, taught with authority, and gave the people He met great hope. Jesus was the promised hope Israel had longed for and the fulfillment of the promise God had given ages ago.

Why did He end up nailed to a cross between two criminals, suffering the most excruciating death imaginable? Why would God allow His perfect Son to be hung on a cross and ridiculed? How could God allow the One who was supposed to rescue Israel to die? Because God had a much bigger plan to save all humanity from the bondage of sin and death. Looking back at the whole picture, we see the events beautifully woven together to bring us our eternal salvation. To the people who followed Jesus, though, the events at the time seemed hopeless. It appeared all was lost.

Stay on the Path

Here we find the two men on the road to Emmaus, on a journey they did not understand. Confused by all that had just happened in Jerusalem, discouraged because their Lord and Savior had just been killed. Walking a road, trying to sort everything out, uncertain of the future. This was more than a pothole. To them, it was the end of the road.

Right now, you may find yourself walking down a seemingly hopeless road. Remember Hebrews 12:1-3:

> *Therefore, since we are surrounded by such a great cloud of witnesses, let us throw off everything that hinders and the sin that so easily entangles. And let us run with perseverance the race marked out for us, fixing our eyes on Jesus, the pioneer and perfecter of our faith. For the joy set before him he endured the cross, scorning its shame, and sat down at the right hand of the throne of God. Consider him who endured such opposition from sinners, so that you will not grow weary and lose heart.*

Fix your eyes on Jesus, not the condition of the road. Persevere, remembering that He endured the cross so that you would be enabled to walk this road. Don't lose heart. God has something extraordinary in store for you that you can't even imagine.

Continue to walk with me along the road to Emmaus, and you will see how beauty unfolds from the dust of this difficult road.

JOURNAL YOUR JOURNEY

Consider Psalm 40:2: "He lifted me out of the slimy pit, out of the mud and mire; he set my feet on a rock and gave me a firm place to stand." Take some time to write about when God lifted you out of the mud and mire and gave you a firm place to stand. Describe the details and thank Him for His goodness.

Maybe you feel like you are still in the mud and mire. Perhaps you are in a pothole of life and can't seem to find your way out of it. Write a prayer asking God to show you the bigger picture, His purpose for your pain. Then remember to fix your eyes on Him, not the road's condition.

JOURNEY THROUGH THE BOOK

1. Put yourself in the shoes of the men on the road to Emmaus as they walked. What would you have been thinking and feeling?

2. In what ways did Joseph focus on God instead of the condition of his road?

3. In what ways did Jesus keep His eyes focused on the Father instead of His circumstances throughout His life?

JOURNEY THROUGH SCRIPTURE

Meditate on the following passages to keep your focus on Jesus:
- Romans 8:28
- Psalm 40:2
- Hebrews 12:1-3

2

Talk to Each Other

They were talking with each other about everything that had happened (Luke 24:14).

Talking with each other is one of the most powerful helps we can experience. Never underestimate the help that other Christians can give you. As humans, we tend to live in a bubble. We don't want to share our weaknesses with others because we fear what they might think. If we admit we are struggling, we believe our faith isn't strong enough, or we don't trust God enough. All of that is a lie from the devil. Many times our weakness is an opportunity to rely on God.

In 2 Corinthians 12:9-10, the Bible tells us that our strength is found in God alone. It says:

But he said to me, "My grace is sufficient for you, for my power is made perfect in weakness." Therefore I will boast all the more gladly about my weaknesses, so that Christ's power may rest on me. That is why, for Christ's sake, I delight in weaknesses, in insults, in hardships, in persecutions, in difficulties. For when I am weak, then I am strong.

When we are at our weakest, God's strength can shine through. Also, we are created with a need to be built up by others. Galatians 6:2 instructs us to "carry each other's burdens,

11

and in this way you will fulfill the law of Christ." Don't be afraid to share your hardships with others in the body of Christ. That is why God gave us our spiritual family. But use discretion in choosing the person(s) you share with. Choose only those you know you can trust and those who will be honest with you.

My Journey

For years, I wasn't living out the teaching above. I didn't tell anyone, even those I grew closest to, the story about my first pregnancy. What most people found joy in talking about—their wedding and the birth of their children—only brought me feelings of shame, embarrassment, and anxiety. I would never ever publicly celebrate my anniversary. I was not prepared to face the questions that came with that announcement.

If I had only known then how powerful it is to open up to others in my time of struggle, I would never have stayed there for as long as I did. The fear of what people would think of me kept me from accepting the freedom that Jesus had for me.

When I finally told my story in a small group setting, a group that included some of my closest friends, I was amazed at their response. They said, "You have to know that God took that from you the moment you received Him," and "There is no judgment here. We're all sinners." What a relief it was to have such a great Christian family! Their response taught me that God uses the gift of people—His family—to talk to and share our struggles with.

Created for Each Other

We were created with a need for companionship. Genesis

2:18-24 says, "It is not good for the man to be alone. I will make a helper suitable for him." From the beginning, God knew that living in isolation without companionship was not good. So, He looked around at all His creation but did not find a suitable helper. That's when He created Eve, taken from Adam's rib, described by Adam as "bone of my bones and flesh of my flesh."

Eve was the perfect companion, another human being—someone to share this journey called life. After falling short of what God commanded and committing the first sin, Eve became someone with whom he could share his struggles and grief. Someone who understood his pain and hardships because she shared the same experiences and failures—a suitable helper, a companion.

Knowing that need is in each one of us, let's look at the two men on their journey to Emmaus. They were talking to each other. They were confused. They didn't understand why circumstances had turned out the way they did. So, they turned to each other, sharing ideas about the future. They must have found strength and comfort in openly talking with each other. After experiencing the worst time of their lives, they had nowhere to turn except each other. So, they walked together and talked it out.

Allow God into Your Discussions

Be careful, though, who you talk to and what the conversation holds. The one thing these men didn't do (at least not yet) was include the Lord in their discussion. While God gave us this wonderful gift of other people, we must be careful not only to talk with those who will tell us only what we want to hear. Remember Proverbs 3:5-6,

Trust in the Lord with all your heart and lean not on your own understanding; in all your ways acknowledge Him, and He will make your paths straight.

When talking with others, always lean on the Lord and not what you think is right. Why were these two men downcast and confused? They had their own ideas of how the events in Jerusalem should have happened. They were leaning on their own understanding. They didn't think about what God might be doing as they talked.

A clear example is included in Mark 9 of the misunderstanding we can get into when we talk to each other and rely on our own understanding. In Mark 9:33-34, the disciples argued about who was the greatest among them. They had clearly taken Jesus out of the conversation and were trying to work out, according to human standards, who the "best" disciple was. Jesus turned this conversation around in verses 35-37. Teaching the disciples what it really means to be great, He also showed us how wrong we will be when we rely only on human understanding. He explained the danger of talking with others with wrong motives—the peril of trying to figure things out without looking for His perspective.

On the contrary, when we invite the Lord into our conversations, talking things out with other people is healthy and necessary. Sometimes it is impossible to understand life's difficulties on our own. Sometimes a burden is simply too heavy to carry alone. That is when we call on other trustworthy Christians and talk to them as we walk down our life's road. We seek godly counsel to walk us through our difficulties. These conversations do not have to fix the problem. Instead, the purpose is to gain strength by fellowshipping with others who understand God is always in control, even when we don't understand.

Share Your Burdens

We are called to encourage one another and build each other up (1 Thessalonians 5:11). We cannot possibly do that unless we share our burdens and triumphs. When life seems confusing and uncertain, these are the best times to get together and discuss what is happening. We should seek out those people who are mature in their faith and grounded in Scripture. They will encourage us with their wisdom, offer ideas we would never have thought of ourselves, and impart strength.

But don't be fooled. Satan will tell you that other people don't want to hear about your problems—that your problem is insignificant compared with others. Remember in those times that Satan is the father of lies. Lying is his native tongue (John 8:44), and his desire is to remove you from the fellowship of believers and isolate you. Do not allow him to steal what God has given you—a family of Christians who provide support and encouragement.

Look again at the men on the road to Emmaus. Remember that while these men were talking and gaining insight, they were still uncertain. They were still confused. Chatting with each other brought comfort, but they still didn't understand all that had happened. It was not until the Lord stepped in later that their eyes were opened.

Don't expect everything to be fixed when you discuss your problems with another believer. Expect comfort, compassion, sound advice, and encouragement, but not necessarily the end to the confusion. You will have to wait on the Lord to find perfect peace from the turmoil. Jesus is the only One who can step in and reveal His will and bring clarity. Other believers can give you the strength to endure the confusion until that clarity comes.

In the waiting, we have each other. During the trial, we have the encouragement of other believers. Don't walk this road alone. Find a companion who will walk by your side, someone you can talk to in your time of need and waiting. And be that person for others. Be a listening ear when someone else is on a road that has them struggling and confused. Even if that is all you can offer—a listening ear—be there for others to talk to and get encouragement from.

Example from the Early Church

Consider the believers in Acts 1:14 and Acts 2:42-47. "They all joined together constantly in prayer," and

> *They devoted themselves to the apostles' teaching and to fellowship, to the breaking of bread and to prayer . . . Every day they continued to meet together in the temple courts. They broke bread in their homes and ate together with glad and sincere hearts.*

Focus on these keywords: constantly, devoted, fellowship, prayer, every day.

This group of believers knew the importance of meeting together and did not neglect it. They knew that if they were going to stay strong in the Lord, they needed each other. These meetings were not just church services where they sang a few songs, listened to a message, and went their separate ways. No, these believers got involved in each other's lives. They were devoted. They made it a point to fellowship and pray together.

This became especially important during the difficult time when Peter was imprisoned. Two small verses tucked into Acts 12 tell us much about the way the early church behaved. Verse 5 tells us the church earnestly prayed for Peter while he was incarcerated. Verse 12 shows that the believers were praying for Peter, and many gathered in the same house to pray.

They undoubtedly remembered Jesus' teaching in Matthew 18:19-20 that He would be there wherever two or three were gathered in His name. Remember, they didn't have the New Testament to read and guide them as we do. Many witnessed Jesus teaching this principle, and now they were living it out. They saw the result of their prayer when Peter knocked at the door and told them about how God had rescued him.

Fellowship with Each Other

At all times, be obedient to Hebrews 10:24-25:

And let us consider how we may spur one another on toward love and good deeds, not giving up meeting together, as some are in the habit of doing, but encouraging one another—and all the more as you see the Day approaching.

Especially when you don't understand, do not neglect meeting together. Make it a point to attend church, prayer meetings, Sunday school, or any place where you can meet with other believers and talk to them.

This is most important when you don't feel like meeting together. It is those times when Satan can most easily infiltrate your thoughts and keep you away from other believers. Don't give him that foothold (Ephesians 4:27). Determine ahead of time that you will not allow Satan to steal the joy you have of being in fellowship with your God-given family of believers. During the most challenging times, do not neglect your need to be with that family.

The Lord has given you this excellent resource—other believers. Talk to them, share your burdens, and walk this road of life alongside other Christians. Be vulnerable with each

17

other. Don't always expect a clear answer or a solution to your problem, but give and receive comfort and encouragement as your fellow believers walk with you and talk to you.

Clarity will come one day, and the Lord will reveal why you had to walk this part of the road. Indeed, the day may not come until you stand face-to-face with the Lord. Many things we just won't understand until we enter His glory. While you wait, struggle, and are confused, surround yourself with His family and walk the road with the encouragement and support they can give.

Stay on this road to Emmaus with me. The journey has just begun, and we have much more to learn as we travel together.

JOURNAL YOUR JOURNEY

Read 1 Thessalonians 5:11: "Therefore encourage one another and build each other up, just as in fact you are doing." Write about a time when you needed someone to talk to, and God sent just the right person who understood and could relate to you. Give the specifics of your situation and conversation, and thank God for that person.

Write a prayer asking God to send the right people into your life at opportune times to help you through the potholes of life. Thank Him in advance for sending these people. Tell Him about what you are going through now and pray for that Christian mentor you need.

JOURNEY THROUGH THE BOOK

1. When have you desperately needed to talk to someone about what you are going through? How did talking to someone encourage your heart?

2. What are the dangers of talking with someone without inviting the Lord in?

3. Knowing Satan's strategy to keep you in isolation, what can you do to recognize his lies and forbid them to rule your heart?

JOURNEY THROUGH SCRIPTURE

Meditate on the following passages to keep your focus on Jesus:
- 2 Corinthians 12:9-10
- Galatians 6:2
- 1 Thessalonians 5:11

3

Jesus in Our Midst

As they talked and discussed these things with each other, Jesus himself came up and walked along with them, but they were kept from recognizing him (Luke 24:15-16).

The two men were walking along the dusty road, and another joined them—the resurrected Jesus. We know from Scripture that the men were kept from recognizing Jesus. Why? We don't know for sure, but we can remember that we have this wonderful promise from the Lord: "For where two or three gather in my name, there am I with them" (Matthew 18:20).

When we gather and talk with each other, Jesus is with us. He will enter the conversation if we let Him. And that is when everything changes. All our own ideas melt away as He gives us clarity of mind. We share ideas with each other that could only come from the risen Lord. Remember that even though Jesus is there, we don't always recognize Him. This was the case for the two men on the road to Emmaus.

Another instance when Jesus entered the scene unrecognized is found in John 20:11-15. Mary Magdalene had gone to the tomb and found it empty She stood crying in distress and grief, wondering who could have taken Jesus' body and why someone would do something so terrible. This was grief on top of grief. Her sorrow was so heavy from watching Jesus die; now, she couldn't even find closure because His body was gone. How would she go on? Where would she go from here? Then Jesus entered her grief, and everything changed. She didn't realize it was Jesus who approached her; she thought He was the gardener. In her deep agony, Mary Magdalene didn't recognize her Savior. Jesus knew her pain and was willing to enter it, even if she didn't recognize Him at first. He is willing to do the same for us.

Unlike the men on the road to Emmaus or Mary Magdalene, we always have Jesus with us. Mary and the two men had not yet experienced the indwelling of the Holy Spirit, so they were confined to talking with Jesus only when He was physically present. No wonder they felt hopeless and confused. They could no longer talk with Jesus. He was no longer there to teach and guide them—or so they thought.

But another man entered the scene on the road to Emmaus, a third companion to walk with them on their journey. But they didn't recognize Him. In fact, they were kept from recognizing Him.

My Journey

I am eternally grateful for the indwelling of the Holy Spirit and that as New Testament believers, we have Jesus present with us all the time. During the period when I clutched my guilt and shame, I know Jesus was with me, even in times I couldn't feel His presence. I didn't realize it at the time, but I know now He drew me back into a church family after I had strayed away. He allowed me to struggle through attending churches where I didn't feel welcome so He could lead me to the family who was exactly right for me.

I know He was the One who led me to repent and turn back to Him after living life my own way. And I know He was always there, walking beside me while I hid my past. He didn't want me to feel lost and humiliated. Looking back, I can see that. In His perfect love, He helped me walk through those feelings of shame and regret in my own time and His perfect timing.

We Fail To Recognize Him

When I read the account of the men not recognizing Jesus on the road to Emmaus, I see two applications that God wants us to learn. First, how quick we are to walk ahead and not recognize the presence of our Savior right there beside us. So often, as we try to figure life out, we make our own decisions and then ask God to bless them instead of asking God first and then acting.

When life gets confusing and complicated, our road fills with gaps we can't steer around. How often do we try to navigate on our own, only turning to Jesus when we land in such a deep hole that we can't crawl out on our own. How often we talk out problems with each other, and Jesus is right there, waiting to join the conversation, but we take no notice of Him.

Jesus is always right beside us, and we fail to recognize Him. He is always waiting for us to invite Him into our walk to guide and direct us, and we overlook Him. Hearing that may make you feel guilty but don't let it discourage you. Jesus knows that in our most challenging times, our vision gets clouded. But you see, Jesus is also working on our behalf even when we don't realize it.

We often don't understand how the little pieces of our lives are being placed together as part of His larger puzzle, creating a beautiful picture we can't see. As noted in the first chapter, a more significant purpose is at play than we recognize. However, we must acknowledge times when we should've seen Jesus but didn't look for Him. We must ask the Lord to open our eyes to see what He is doing.

Consider Elisha and his servant in 1 Kings 6:15-17. Elisha's servant looked around, and all he could see was a sizable army surrounding them. He was filled with fear and didn't know what to do. The situation looked hopeless, with no way to escape such a large, powerful army. But Elisha could see an even bigger army that God had provided. So, Elisha prayed to the Lord that his servant's eyes would be opened. The servant saw a multitude of chariots and horses of fire all around them on the hillsides.

The Lord's army had been there all along, but in his fear, the servant failed to recognize it. Once his eyes were opened, the fear left because he could see the work of the living God. We too can pray for our eyes to be opened. Jesus is always right beside us, walking this road with us. Pray that your eyes will be opened to see Him.

We Are Kept From Recognizing Him

The second application I see is that sometimes we are not ready to come face-to-face with the living God. You see, the two men on the road to Emmaus were kept from recognizing Jesus. I was confused by that fact at first. The resurrected Christ walked with them. Wouldn't He want to be identified so they would believe in Him? As it turns out, the men had to get their hearts in the right place before they could see Jesus. They needed the Scripture explained to them so they could see the purpose behind everything they had just experienced in

Jerusalem. They simply were not ready to face Jesus, and Jesus knew that.

We are very much like these men. Many times the Lord needs to soften our hearts so we can see Him clearly. Especially in times of confusion and disappointment, Jesus is patient with us and allows us to walk without recognizing Him. But all the while, He is walking beside us, feeding us the little bits of manna we need to get our hearts in the right place to receive what He has to show us.

He knows just the right time to reveal Himself and open our eyes. He loves us too much to show anything before we are prepared to receive it. So, He lovingly walks beside us until we are ready. He waits patiently for our hearts to soften to His voice. Remember Mary in John 20? Jesus allowed her to pour out her grief, and then, at the right time, He said, "Mary."

Knowing that we serve a God who knows so much about us is remarkable. How much peace we can have, knowing that our Savior cares about us so much He is even willing to keep us from recognizing His presence for a brief time. When the time is right, He will amaze us. We serve an amazing God who knows exactly what we need and when we need it. He even knows when and if our hearts are ready to receive what He has to teach us. How comforting to know that Jesus will always be with us, even when we overlook Him.

God Is Always Present

Multiple Scriptures tell us that God is always with us. Here are just a few for you to ponder:

- Deuteronomy 31:6, 8 – God will never leave you or forsake you.

24

- Joshua 1:5 – Again, He will never leave you or forsake you.
- Joshua 1:9 – The Lord will be with you wherever you go.
- 1 Chronicles 28:20 – God will never fail you or forsake you.
- Psalm 73:23-24 – God is always with you; He holds you by the hand and guides you.
- Isaiah 41:10 – God strengthens you and helps you; He holds you by the hand.
- Matthew 28:20 – God is with you always.
- Hebrews 13:5 – God says again, "I will never leave you or forsake you."

I am convinced that the Lord repeats statements in His Word numerous times because He wants us to pay special attention to them. Take some time to think about what these verses say to you. Read them and reread them and let them sink into your heart. Say them out loud and claim them as truth. Turn to them again and again when you are experiencing challenges and can't feel His presence. May these passages of Scripture bring you comfort. May you always realize that Jesus is right there with you. He promises to never leave you or forsake you. Even when you don't recognize Him, He is there and always will be.

So, don't get discouraged when you feel stuck in your grief, when you are so filled with sadness and confusion that you can't see God. Tuck this truth in your heart: Jesus is always there, and He knows your pain. Jesus has never left your side. He will walk beside you, even when you don't recognize Him, and He will lovingly wait until you are ready to see Him. When your eyes are opened, you will be amazed at what Jesus will show you. He always has perfect beauty awaiting you, and He will reveal it in His perfect timing.

That is what the men on the road to Emmaus had to learn. At the very lowest point of their lives, Jesus was right there. They didn't recognize Him, but He was there. Later, Jesus would reveal Himself, and the joy that sprung from that moment was like no other. For now, He was allowing them the time and space to understand and receive what He had to show them. Jesus patiently taught them the lesson that He would never leave or forsake them. Out of His perfect love, He was waiting for the right moment to reveal Himself and change their lives forever.

We too must learn this lesson. We can declare with our mouths and acknowledge in our minds that Jesus is always there, but we must let it sink into the depths of our hearts. We must grab onto His promises as absolute, unwavering truth. Like the men on the road to Emmaus, He will patiently teach us that lesson. Sometimes that means waiting to reveal Himself until our hearts are ready.

Don't give up when you can't see Jesus. Keep moving forward. Continue to walk this journey in the coming chapters, listening for His sweet voice. You will see just how perfectly God cares for you, how deeply He loves you, and how wonderfully He works out His plan for you.

Journal Your Journey

Read Joshua 1:9: "Have I not commanded you? Be strong and courageous. Do not be afraid; do not be discouraged, for the Lord your God will be with you wherever you go." Journal about a time you needed strength and courage, and you had it, even though you were having trouble sensing God's presence. Thank Him for His goodness and faithfulness to never leave your side.

Maybe you are experiencing a time right now when you don't feel very strong or courageous. Write a prayer asking God to show Himself to you, to help you sense His presence in your situation.

Journey through the Book

1. What comfort do you get knowing that Jesus will be there when you fellowship with other believers?

2. Think of how prone you are to try to solve problems, even small ones, yourself. Why do we sometimes act on our own and not look for Jesus right away?

3. Do you think that maybe the men were kept from seeing Jesus so that He could work in their hearts, so that they could process their feelings?

Journey through Scripture

Meditate on the following passages to keep your focus on Jesus:
* Matthew 18:20
* Joshua 1:5
* Isaiah 41:10

4

We Are Downcast

He asked them, "What are you discussing together as you walk along?" They stood still, their faces downcast" (Luke 24:17).

Here was the moment that Jesus invited Himself into the conversation. Knowing full well what they were talking about, He used a simple question, "What is it that you're discussing?" This simple question is more profound than it looks on the surface. Nothing is a mystery to God. He knows our every thought (Psalm 139:2).

In the case of these two men walking to Emmaus, Jesus couldn't wait to open the Scriptures to them and reveal the truth about what they had just gone through in Jerusalem. He longed to show them the perfect plan that had unfolded. Jesus was excited to announce that He had conquered death forever, but He gave them the chance to process their feelings and be ready to hear what He had to say.

As was addressed in the last chapter, Jesus knows us so well that He knows when we are ready to receive a word from Him and when we are not. He always invites us to talk to Him about what we are going through. Even with Mary Magdalene in the garden in John 20, the first words Jesus said were, "Why are you crying?"

He could have revealed Himself immediately, but instead, He allowed Mary Magdalene to express her grief. He asks the simple question, "What's troubling you?" or "What's on your mind?" And we can tell Him. He already knows our answer, but He also knows we must get it off our chests. When a situation eats away at our minds, the best thing we can do is talk about it, and the best One to talk to is Jesus.

My Journey

I had a moment like this on my journey. Before I heard from Jesus Himself, I had a dear lady in Christ step into my pain and lead me in the direction I needed to go. In 2010, my husband and I decided to attend Marriage Encounter's weekend retreat. I thought we were there to make our marriage flourish, and we were, but little did I know God had a much bigger plan for healing my heart.

As retreat speakers, a pastor and his wife told how their daughter was found to be pregnant outside of wedlock. They spoke of the shame they felt. There they were, a pastoral couple, leading a church, and their daughter fell into this sin. What would their congregation think? How could they face them? Then they shared how their church family wrapped their arms around them and treated them with compassion and grace. I cried and cried throughout their whole story. It was as if they were telling my story to me.

After the session, while I was in the hallway drying my eyes, the wife came to talk to me. She simply asked, "What's troubling you?" The tears flowed again. The gracious woman was able to speak with me and help me understand that I had no reason to be living in this state of shame. Jesus had taken care of that at the cross. This was the first time in six years that

I had spoken out loud to anyone about my past. An incredible weight lifted off my shoulders at that moment. My freedom all started with a simple question. I believe that Jesus spoke to me through that beautiful woman, and I am forever grateful to her for being obedient to come to find me. Her simple question changed my life.

The Perfect Love of Christ

Notice that Jesus did the same thing with the men on the road to Emmaus. When He approached these men, He didn't step in and start explaining things immediately. Instead, Jesus lovingly asked a simple question. He allowed them room to express their feelings, giving them the space to explain things from their perspective, flawed as it was. Jesus knew they were confused and didn't understand their circumstances. He also knew their human minds needed time to process all that they had just experienced.

We often want Jesus to step into our circumstances and fix things right away. Still, He knows so much more than we do. He knows how our brains work and what needs to happen to find healing. We need time to think through and process our hurts, and Jesus gives us that time.

We see the processing in the following sentence: "They stood still, their faces downcast" (Luke 24:17). Here they were, with the resurrected Jesus in their midst, and their faces were dejected. It had only been three days since they watched their Lord die a brutal death, and their minds had not yet wrapped around all that had happened. They could not yet understand how and why God would allow this terrible thing to occur. They were overwhelmed with the grief of what happened in Jerusalem, and what that meant for the rest of their lives. They couldn't imagine a future now that all their hopes, dreams, and plans had been ruined in such a short time. They had believed Jesus was the Messiah, but now that He had died, they had no idea how to move forward.

Life sometimes puts us in this situation when a loved one dies, we lose our job, or we experience a house fire or car accident. Maybe somebody we trust stabs us in the back, or we are forced to deal with the numerous other difficulties life throws us. Life is unpredictable and can become jagged and full of potholes that impede our progress. Sometimes those potholes fill with mud so thick that we get stuck, and it seems like we will never crawl out of it. The situation becomes so overwhelming, and we are so overcome with grief that we stand still with our faces downcast like the men on the road to Emmaus. We can't imagine what to do or where to go from here. Time seems to stop, and we can't see hope for the future.

Then Jesus steps in and says, "Child, what is bothering you?" Instead of immediately rescuing us from our situation, He lovingly initiates a conversation. He allows us time and space to grieve. But remember, He has been standing with you and walking with you the entire time, even when you're depressed, and it seems there are no answers. He has never left you. When you think He's not answering, remember that He might be waiting for you to process the trauma you just experienced. He is saying, "Talk to Me. Tell Me what's on your mind."

Honesty with Your Savior

Don't be afraid to be honest when you answer His question. He already knows what you're thinking. He also knows how valuable verbalizing your pain is. So, tell Him. That's what the two men on the road to Emmaus did. Before looking at what the men said to Jesus, ponder how big the love of Jesus is to allow you to go through the grieving process and not rush it.

Consider Mary and Martha in John 11:1-44. Lazarus, their brother and good friend of Jesus, had died. They knew that if Jesus only would have been there, He could have prevented his death. In fact, Jesus had known that Lazarus was sick, yet He waited two days before going to see him. Lazarus had been in the tomb for four days by the time Jesus arrived. The Lord met with Mary and Martha separately, but the conversation was the same. They both said to Him, "If you would have been here, my brother would not have died" (John 11:21, 32) Jesus Himself wept over the death of His friend.

The Lord knew He would show the gathered crowd God's glory by raising Lazarus from the dead. Instead of rushing into the miracle, He gave Mary and Martha moments to grieve the tragedy of their brother's death. Jesus allowed them to voice their feelings and begin to process their grief. Amid their pain, He taught them a valuable lesson. He is the resurrection and the life. Anyone who believes in Him will never die.

Another example of Jesus allowing someone to express their feelings is in John 5:1-9. In this case, the man expressed frustration at his condition and even showed some self-pity. Again, instead of just stepping in to fix the problem, Jesus asked a simple question, "Do you want to get well?" (v. 6). Although I hate to admit it, the man's answer reflects how I often feel. Instead of saying, "Yes, Lord, I want to get well!" the man started to tell a sob story about how all his efforts had failed because nobody would help him.

How often, in our confusion, grief, and frustration, do we

respond the same way! But Jesus didn't rebuke or reprimand the man for reacting that way. In love, He was providing the man room and permission to express how he really felt. Then the healing came. No punishment for feeling frustrated, no guilt for feeling sorry for himself, just pure and complete recovery.

This is one part of the reason to process your grief and pain—to realize that no matter what happens or how bleak the circumstances look, we can rely on Jesus. He always has your life under control. He is the ultimate healer, the One who guarantees our eternal life. Unless we have the time to ponder and walk through our grief, we will never completely understand Jesus' goodness.

When our faces are downcast, and we take the time to sit still, Jesus asks us, "What are you thinking? Bring it to Me and let Me heal it." Then He gives us time to answer Him. He gives us permission to be totally honest before Him and talk out everything we think and feel. Remember 1 Peter 5:7 when you are grieving: "Cast all your anxiety on Him because He cares for you." Then worship your loving Savior, the One who knows what you need at precisely the right time.

Stay on the Path

Walk with the men on the road to Emmaus in the following few chapters. We will break down the conversation between these men and Jesus and see how we can have the same type of conversation with Him. The men could tell Jesus exactly how they felt, and Jesus simply allowed them the space to do that. He didn't interrupt; He didn't try to tell them they were wrong; He just let them feel what they were feeling and express it to Him. If you stick with them further down the road, you'll see that it was never Jesus' intention to leave them in their grief and confusion but to show Himself powerfully.

Take comfort in the fact that Jesus will do the same for you. He will gently whisper to you, "What are you talking about as you walk along the road?" He will allow you to come to Him with all your pain, sorrow, and confusion. When you give your problems to Him, He will lovingly walk you through your situation. Stay on the road, dusty as it may be, and wait for His perfect timing.

Journal Your Journey

Reflect on 1 Peter 5:7: "Cast all your anxiety on him because he cares for you." Think of a time when you were discouraged because of your circumstances. Maybe that time is right now. Write about what you need to do to give your anxiety and grief to God. Thank Him for being willing to take it from you.

Write a prayer asking God what you're holding on to that you need to give to Him. Ask Him to show you how to relinquish the confusion, grief, and sadness to Him.

Journey through the Book

1. How does it make you feel that Jesus, who is all-powerful and all-knowing, is willing to ask you the simple question, "What's troubling you?"

2. Close your eyes and imagine Jesus approaching you and saying, "Child, what is bothering you?" Express how that makes you feel and how you would answer Him.

3. Follow through on this quote from earlier in this chapter: "Ponder how big the love of Jesus is to allow you to go through the grieving process and not rush it." Write the thoughts that come to your mind as you do this.

Journey through Scripture

Meditate on the following passages to keep your focus on Jesus:
- John 11:14-15
- John 5:1-9
- 1 Peter 5:7

5

Don't You Get It, God?

One of them, named Cleopas, asked him, "Are you the only one visiting Jerusalem who does not know the things that have happened there in these days?" (Luke 24:18)

Because the men on the road to Emmaus didn't yet know they were talking to the risen Lord, the men were taken aback when Jesus asked them what they were talking about. Who was this man, and how could He possibly not know all the things that just happened in Jerusalem?

Everyone in Jerusalem and all the surrounding areas knew about Jesus being crucified. It was the news of the day. Everyone was talking about it. How could this guy not know what had happened? You can almost hear the sarcasm in Cleopas's voice. To put it in modern terms, he said, "Dude, do you seriously not get it? How could you have been in Jerusalem and not know what went on? You can't be serious."

How much like these men we are when talking to God! We know that God knows everything, sees everything, and is everywhere. We know that He hears and answers our prayers. When tragedy strikes, however, God can seem to be silent. Even when we understand that He wants us to bring our hurts to Him, we still want to cry out in our grief, "Don't You get it,

God? Don't You see my hurt?" We desperately want Him to heal our wounds, and we don't know what to do. When things don't seem to be getting any better, or maybe even worse, it is in our very nature to say, "Don't You get it, God? Can't You see my pain? Don't You know how they've treated me?"

My Journey

I had moments of saying, "Don't You get it, God?" before I found the courage to open up to my church family about my past. I would say things to Him such as, "Don't You see, they will all look at me differently if I tell them about my past. Everyone will think I'm a fake, just acting like a Christian on the outside."

But the truth was, I continued to live in my shame because the father of lies, the devil, had infiltrated my thoughts. While I was crying out, "Don't You get it, God?" Satan was telling me that the relationships I had built with my church family would be ruined if I told them about my sin. They would never look at me in the same way. They would think less of me. I couldn't possibly be a good Christian in their eyes if they knew my secret.

Of course, I know now that my scars were caused by those ladies at the first church I visited. I don't hold anything against them. I know God allowed me to hear their conversation as part of my journey to find healing from my guilt and shame. While their words hurt and left me struggling, through that experience I learned what it means to be a "good" Christian— someone who can say, "That is who I was, but this is who I am now." A good Christian recognizes that we are nothing without Christ, and once we are found in Him, guilt and shame are no more. Instead, we boast in the Lord about what He's accomplished.

The Israelites' Struggle

Let's look at what the Israelites went through in the time after Joseph rescued Egypt from famine. In Exodus 1, a new Pharoah took the throne in Egypt. The Israelite nation had become quite large, and this new king felt threatened. Because he didn't know Joseph, and Joseph meant nothing to him (Exodus 1:8), the Israelites were put into slavery. Even worse, the midwives were told to kill all the male babies so the Israeli population would decrease. In Exodus 2:23, the people cried out to God in their slavery but did not get an immediate answer. The cry probably went something like this, "Don't You see us, God? We are Your chosen people, yet here we are enslaved in a foreign land. Why are You allowing this to happen to us? Don't You get it, God?"

Along came Moses in Exodus 3 and 4. God had told him to tell Pharaoh to let His people go. Keep in mind that the Israelites didn't know anything about this burning bush experience at the time. God was working out a plan even while they were still living in slavery, but they couldn't see that. They had no way of knowing that soon someone would speak on their behalf. They had no idea how God would work in their distress. Their misery was so great that they probably couldn't see any way out of it. So, their cry of anguish was still rising up before God, and there was no way for them to understand why they still suffered or how it would end. "Don't You get it, God? Can't You see we're suffering? Why won't You rescue us?"

Even Moses had a "Don't you get it, God?" moment. When God told Moses to tell Pharaoh to let His people out of Egypt, Moses had many reasons why he couldn't do it. Read through Exodus 3 and 4 to see the whole story. I paraphrase Moses' conversation with God: "Don't You get it, God? They won't listen to me. I'm a nobody. Why would they believe You sent me? Don't You know me, God? I'm not an eloquent speaker. I can't talk before Pharaoh. Come on, Lord, there must be someone else."

God answered each question: "Yes, Moses, I do get it. You are not capable to do this on your own. That's why I will be with you. I will enable you to accomplish the task that I've set before you, and I will help you." Moses had to understand God's promise to never leave or forsake him. He had to struggle through moments of doubt and feelings of inadequacy before God could use him for this tremendous task He had set before him.

In Exodus 5, Moses obeyed the call. He went to Pharaoh and said that God commanded that the king let the people of Israel go. What happened? Pharaoh made the slave labor harder on the Israelites. He took away the straw for making bricks and made them find their own straw yet still required the same quota of bricks to be produced.

Naturally, the Israelites went to Moses and said (again, I'm paraphrasing), "Thanks a lot. Your big mouth has just made things worse for us. You've set us up so that Pharaoh can work us to death. This is all your fault." Moses then had another "Don't You get it, God?" moment. In Exodus 5:22-23, he said, "Why, Lord, why have you brought trouble on this people? Is this why you sent me? Ever since I went to Pharaoh to speak in your name, he has brought trouble on this people, and You have not rescued Your people at all." Do you hear the anguish in Moses' voice? Why, Lord? Don't You get it, God?

Our Struggle

We are just like the Israelites and Moses. Like the Israelites, we desperately want an end to our pain, anguish, and grief. When we can't see how God is working things out, we cry, "Don't You get it, God?" Like Moses, when we are called to do something that we feel inadequate to do, we say to God, "Don't You know me? I can't do that." When we are obedient, and things don't work out like we expect them to, we ask, "Why, God?"

Then like the men on the road to Emmaus, we are discouraged. We start to doubt the goodness of God. We wonder if what we were called to do really came from Him. We allow the father of lies into our thoughts. Satan's influence makes us feel hopeless and helpless, and our faces reflect our sadness.

We need to read the end of the story in times like these. God was with Moses. The Lord was working out His perfect plan for the Israelites and teaching them to trust Him along the way. He is doing the same for us. We need to remember His promise to never leave us or forsake us. God did free the Israelites from their bondage in His perfect timing. Israel's rescue didn't come right away, though. It took ten plagues to break through Pharaoh's hard heart. Moses had to remain steadfastly obedient, even when he was frustrated. God will rescue us from our suffering and bondage, but He will do it in His time, not ours.

Struggling for a Purpose

Consider the apostle Paul in 2 Corinthians 12:6-10. Paul was given a "thorn in his flesh" to help him from becoming prideful in His walk with Christ. No one is certain what this thorn was, but I can tell you it was something miserable. Paul said he "pleaded" three times for God to take it away. I imagine Paul was having a "Don't You get it, God?" moment. There he was, sitting in misery, begging for his thorn to be taken away, but God responded, "My grace is sufficient for you." Sometimes that is the answer we need to hear in our suffering.

God doesn't always choose to remove the suffering, at least not right away. In those moments, we are tempted to say, "Don't You get it, God?" God lovingly responds, "Of course, I get it, but I want you to see that my grace is sufficient for you." The Lord knows what we need to experience to grow closer to Him. He doesn't enjoy our suffering any more than we do. Still, He knows that He is accomplishing something beautiful in our lives that couldn't happen any other way. His grace is sufficient to see us through it.

Here is one more example to encourage your heart even more. Jesus, knowing that He was headed to the cross, went to the garden of Gethsemane to pray. Luke 22 says that He was in so much anguish that he sweated drops of blood. He cried to God, "Father, if you are willing, take this cup from me; yet not my will, but yours be done" (v. 42). Later, as Jesus hung on the cross, taking on Himself the sin of the whole world, panting for His last breaths so that you and I could have eternal life, He cried out in anguish. Matthew 27:46 says, "About three in the afternoon Jesus cried out in a loud voice, 'Eli, Eli, lema sabachthani?' (which means, "My God, my God, why have you forsaken me?").

Even Jesus, God Incarnate, had to rely on the Father during His times of deepest need and anguish. Although He was fully God, He was also fully human and had suffered the same human emotions and pain we do. When He went to pray at Gethsemane, it was because His Spirit was willing but His flesh was weak (Matthew 26:41). He knew the pain and anguish, both mental and physical, that were about to come, and He knew He couldn't do it without the help of the Father.

But He didn't have to yell, "Don't You get it, God?" He understood the plan, but it was difficult and painful.

We need to approach the Father in the way Jesus did and give our pain to Him. Sometimes all you can say is, "Don't You get it, God?" but you still can go to Him. His love will never leave you in question, and He will not be offended by your confusion and grief. So, tell Him. Let Him know that you are confused, in anguish, afraid, grieving, and unsure of what the future holds. And be confident that the God of the universe does indeed "get it." He will rescue you in His perfect timing. Even, like the Israelites, when things seem to get worse instead of better, He is working out His perfect plan for you. Trust that His grace is sufficient and hold on to the promise that He will never leave or forsake you.

Continue to follow the progress of these two men on the road to Emmaus. Watch their interactions with the risen Savior and see that their route is not so different from ours. We need to slip into their shoes and continue to learn all the brilliant lessons God has for us from this encounter. Walk with these men and experience the love of Jesus along the pathway.

Journal Your Journey

Matthew 26:41 says, "Watch and pray so that you will not fall into temptation. The spirit is willing, but the flesh is weak." Write about how you tend to have the right intentions with God, but your human nature gets in the way. Think about the times you want to shout, "Don't You get it, God?" What is it that makes you feel that way?

Write a prayer asking God to show you that it is okay to question Him when you are doubting and confused. Thank Him that He loves you so much that He allows you to process your pain instead of jumping in to save the day.

Journey through the Book

1. Have you ever had a moment when you said to God, "Don't You get it?" What was happening in your life that made you feel that way?

2. Think about Paul in 2 Corinthians 12:6-10. How has God's grace been sufficient for you?

3. How does seeing Jesus relying on the Father in His times of profound anguish encourage you to do the same?

Journey through Scripture

Meditate on the following passages to keep your focus on Jesus:

- Matthew 26:41
- Exodus 2:23-25
- 2 Corinthians 12:9-10

6

Jesus Wants Us To Share

"What things?" he asked (Luke 24:19).

This is a short line of Scripture, but it has so much to teach us. After the men on the road to Emmaus had their "Don't You get it?" moment, saying, "Don't you know the things that just happened in Jerusalem?" Jesus simply asked, "What things?" Wait a minute. This is Jesus, and it's not even the same Jesus they knew. This is Jesus who has risen from the dead. He is the Jesus who conquered death and sin. Doesn't He know "what things" they are talking about? Of course, He does. So why ask?

First, remember that in the case of these two men, they didn't yet know that they were talking to the risen Lord. Recall from previous chapters that He was giving them the time and space they needed to process their emotions before revealing Himself to them. Remember that He lovingly does that for us as well. Maybe the men didn't know who Jesus was, but He knew. He didn't have to question "what things" happened. He was the One who suffered! But He asked anyway; He wanted them to explain their perspective of what had happened. He wanted to know what was in their hearts.

My Journey

One of the hardest things for me to do on my journey was to speak out loud to the Lord that I was holding on to the guilt and shame that He had already taken care of on the cross. I had to admit to Him that I was living the lie that His grace wasn't sufficient. For a long time, I didn't think I needed to do this. Jesus already knew, right? Why should I have to tell Him something He already knew and for which He had already forgiven me?

It wasn't the sin of having a baby out of wedlock that I needed to disclose. I had done that already. I needed to confess to God that I had allowed Satan to control how I thought about my sin. I had to admit out loud that I was not allowing His grace to manifest in my life. I had to confide that I was letting my fear dominate His grace. I had to tell Him what He already knew to gain the freedom that only He could provide. It was one of the most challenging yet rewarding actions I've ever taken.

Jesus Knows You

Even though Jesus knows everything, even our thoughts, He still wants us to tell Him. He wants to give us the opportunity we so desperately need to voice our hurts to Him. He wants to give us the perfect freedom only He can provide: freedom from guilt and shame, and freedom from grief and sorrow. He doesn't need us to tell Him anything, but He loves us so much that He wants us to speak to Him. This is such a pivotal point to understand. I want to take some time to explore just how well our Lord knows us and why this chance to tell Him everything He already knows is such an act of love.

Let's first look at Psalms 139 to get a picture of just how well God knows us. Verses 1-6 tell us that God knows everything we do, think, and say (even before we say it), and He has His hand on everything. That might sound a little scary and make us pray the words in verses 7-12. Where can I escape from God? Where could I possibly go where He can't find me? But realize that when God sees and knows everything, it is out of pure love, a love that we can't even fathom. Then remember verse 10. His hand is there to guide you, to hold you fast. Not only does God know everything about you, but He also is the One who formed you. Read verses 13-16. Your God created you, He knit you together, and every day of your life was written in His book before one of them came to pass. God knows you better than you know yourself.

God even knows the number of hairs on your head (Matthew 10:30). Think about that. That number is constantly changing. My hairdresser once told me that, on average, people lose about fifty hairs a day. But then more grow back every day. Only God knows how many hairs each of us has on our heads at any given time, something we couldn't possibly know about ourselves. He knows everything about us, and yet He still says, "What things?" He invites us to tell Him what is on our minds, even though He already knows. He invites us to let go of what is weighing us down. He invites us out of the pothole on our road.

One other concept is astonishing! God knew us before He even created the earth. Read that again. Before God said, "Let there be light," He knew you. Ephesians 1:4 says, "For he chose us in him before the creation of the world to be holy and blameless in his sight," and 2 Timothy 1:9 says, "He has saved us and called us to a holy life—not because of anything we have done, but because of his own purpose and grace. This grace was given us in Christ Jesus before the beginning of time."

Wow! The Lord of heaven and earth, Creator of all things, had us on His mind even before anything physical existed. His grace was present before time began, long before we ever needed it, but He knew we would need it, so there it was. This kind of knowledge is unfathomable. Psalm 139:6 says, "Such knowledge is too wonderful for me, too lofty for me to attain." This is a love and an understanding that we cannot comprehend.

Therefore, realize that because God created us and knew us before the beginning of time, He also knows how we process our emotions. After all, He created those too. He knows that when we are hurting deeply, grieving takes time, and our brains that He made need to go through a process for us to come out on the other side healthy. Could the Lord choose to just speak and take away all our pain? Of course. But He loves us so much, and He wants us to lean on Him so heavily that He allows us to go through the process of telling Him and giving it to Him. He wants us to put a voice to all the things that He already knows.

God Is Faithful

Let's return for a moment to the two men on the road to Emmaus. They discussed what had just happened in Jerusalem as they walked along, and their faces were downcast. They had just lost everything and were very distraught about their uncertain future. Jesus knew what they were thinking, feeling, and saying. But He lovingly joined the conversation and didn't jump in to save the day right away. Jesus allowed them to sit in their grief for a little while, talk to Him about it, and process it. He asked them, "What things?" as if He didn't already know. All of this leads me to think about Job. Here was a man who lost everything—his livelihood, family, health—and God didn't come to the rescue immediately. In Job 2:8-9, Job is sitting in a pile of ashes, scraping sores off his skin with a piece of broken pottery, and his wife is telling him to curse God and die. Life doesn't get any lower than that. It seems so cruel for God to allow all of that suffering in the life of a man described in Job 1:1 as "blameless and upright; he feared God and shunned evil." God seems to be absent in Job's suffering until chapter 38. But He was not missing at all. God was allowing something terrible and difficult in Job's life to show him just how faithful He is.

If you read through the entire book of Job, and I encourage you to do just that, you'll see a process that parallels the one the men on the road to Emmaus had. First, you will see a complex and seemingly hopeless situation, followed by discouragement and feeling like there is no hope for the future. Then along came friends to talk to and help him process the grief. Job needed to be careful about talking to friends without making God part of their conversation. Finally, God entered the picture and spoke into the situation. He didn't just swoop in and take all the pain away but allowed time to process what was happening. In Job's case, discipline was involved, but only in love and with knowledge about Job that only God had. At the end of the story, we see the beauty that came out of the ashes.

We haven't reached the end of the walk our two men were on, but we will see this same beauty come out of their hopelessness in the chapters to come, and we can see it in our lives as well. This walk is not always easy, and the road is not always smooth, but God walks with us. Sometimes, instead of straightening the curves or smoothing out the potholes, God says, "What things?" What's bothering you? Why is your face so downcast? He loves us so much that He wants us to speak it out loud, to get it out of our heads and hearts. He wants us to tell Him all of it, not hold anything back, and gain that tremendous perfect freedom found only in Him.

So, remember this: when God allows pain in your life, it is not because He is cruel and unloving. When it seems as though God can't make things better and your future is hopeless, He is allowing space for your mind and emotions to process what is happening. Jesus knows everything, even your deepest pain, yet He still asks, "What things?" He wants you to pour your heart out to Him and give words to your feelings and emotions. Not because He doesn't know what you're going through, but because in His perfect love, He knows what it is you need—time to grieve, process, and talk to Him. And after you do that, you will see the beauty that comes from your pain.

We aren't at the end of the road yet. Just wait and see what Jesus has in store!

JOURNAL YOUR JOURNEY

Read Psalm 139 on the following pages. Write out all the beautiful ways your heavenly Father knows you. Go through each verse and thank Him for the way He created you.

Write a prayer expressing all the things you need to tell God. Thank Him that He already knows, but He wants you to come to Him with all of it.

JOURNEY THROUGH THE BOOK

1. Reading Psalm 139, what thoughts come to mind when you realize just how well God knows you?

2. Think about this quote from the book: "God knew us before He even created the Earth." What kinds of feelings does that stir up within you?

3. Since God could choose to erase our pain immediately, why doesn't He?

JOURNEY THROUGH SCRIPTURE

Meditate on the following passages to keep your focus on Jesus:
- Matthew 10:30
- Ephesians 1:4
- 2 Timothy 1:9

Psalm 139

You have searched me, Lord, and you know me.
You know when I sit and when I rise;
you perceive my thoughts from afar.
You discern my going out and my lying down;
you are familiar with all my ways.
Before a word is on my tongue
you, Lord, know it completely.
You hem me in behind and before,
and you lay your hand upon me.
Such knowledge is too wonderful for me,
too lofty for me to attain.

Where can I go from your Spirit?
Where can I flee from your presence?
If I go up to the heavens, you are there;
if I make my bed in the depths, you are there.
If I rise on the wings of the dawn,
if I settle on the far side of the sea,
even there your hand will guide me,
your right hand will hold me fast.
If I say, "Surely the darkness will hide me
and the light become night around me,"
even the darkness will not be dark to you;
the night will shine like the day,
for darkness is as light to you.

For you created my inmost being;
you knit me together in my mother's womb.

I praise you because I am fearfully and wonderfully made;
your works are wonderful,
I know that full well.

My frame was not hidden from you
when I was made in the secret place,
when I was woven together in the depths of the earth.
Your eyes saw my unformed body;
all the days ordained for me were written in your book
before one of them came to be.
How precious to me are your thoughts, God!
How vast is the sum of them!
Were I to count them,
they would outnumber the grains of sand—
when I awake, I am still with you.

If only you, God, would slay the wicked!
Away from me, you who are bloodthirsty!
They speak of you with evil intent;
your adversaries misuse your name.
Do I not hate those who hate you, Lord,
and abhor those who are in rebellion against you?
I have nothing but hatred for them;
I count them my enemies.

Search me, God, and know my heart;
test me and know my anxious thoughts.
See if there is any offensive way in me,
and lead me in the way everlasting.

7

Not What I Expected

"About Jesus of Nazareth," they replied. "He was a prophet, powerful in word and deed before God and all the people. The chief priests and our rulers handed him over to be sentenced to death, and they crucified him; but we had hoped that he was the one who was going to redeem Israel. And what is more, it is the third day since all this took place" (Luke 24:19-21).

Here it is—the moment of truth. The moment we decide to take Jesus up on His offer to tell Him everything, to explain our grief to Him. What is most often our chief complaint? Circumstances didn't turn out how we thought they would or how we thought they should.

We see God's blessings as only being the good things in life, and we don't realize that often what we think is bad, God is using for good. We have this idea of our future, the expectation that God will order our lives to match our imaginations and dreams. When He doesn't, we are perplexed and confused.

That's where we find the two men on the road to Emmaus in this passage of Scripture. They finally put a voice to all their grief. They spill their guts, and you can hear the hurt in their voices as they do. We hoped Israel would be redeemed through this man Jesus, but instead, He was crucified. All our hopes for the future died with Him on that cross. It's been three days since this happened, and we just don't know what to do. There is no more hope for Israel. Things didn't turn out like we thought they would. This isn't how the story was supposed to end; now we're lost and hopeless. Where do we go from here?

Oh, if only they realized they were talking to Jesus! The hope they so desperately wanted was there, walking beside them, listening to them pour out their grief. How often have we found ourselves in the same situation, pouring our hearts out to God yet still feeling helpless and hopeless? If only we realized that He walked beside us, listening to us pour out our grief.

We need to remember that He knows. He knows our struggles, He knows our despair, and He knows we need to pour it all out at His feet. Even when we don't feel His presence, even when we can't see Him, He is listening, allowing us to voice the turmoil inside us. He is letting us share our confusion and frustration about how things didn't turn out the way we thought they should.

My Journey

I was in this place at one time. In the six years before I attended Marriage Encounter, I wallowed in the muddy pothole of self-pity. Life hadn't turned out the way I thought it would, and it was all my fault. I messed up, and I couldn't make it right again no matter what I did. How could I live a Christian life with this kind of sin in my background? How could I possibly serve the Lord? I was faithfully attending church, but I was afraid someone would find out about my past and change their perception of me.

Mine was not the picture-perfect life I thought it had to be to serve God well. I knew my sin was forgiven, but I also lived as if that didn't matter. Yes, I knew I had eternal life and heaven's assurance, but it wasn't making a difference in my life here on earth. I read about the abundant life in Christ but was not experiencing it. It seemed like everyone else at church had it all together and had lived their entire lives for Jesus. Things just weren't what I thought they should be.

Jonah's Struggle

Jonah had a moment like this. I encourage you to read the whole book of Jonah to get a picture of all his struggles, but we are going to focus on chapter 4. Jonah had preached a message of repentance to the people of Nineveh, and they turned from their wicked ways. That sounds exactly like what Jonah should have wanted, right? After all, that was a prophet's job— share the message of God so that people could understand who He was and change their ways.

I would think he would have felt accomplished. The people listened to his message, heeded God's warning, and turned their lives around. Mission accomplished. However, in Jonah 4:1, we see that Jonah is angry. How could a prophet preach the Word of God, successfully turn a city from its sin, and then be mad about it?

Because Nineveh was a wicked city. Nahum 3:1 describes the town this way: "Woe to the city guilty of bloodshed! She is full of lies; she is filled with plunder; she has hoarded her spoil!" When Jonah was called to Nineveh to preach against its sin, his first response was to run in the other direction. He wanted nothing to do with their wickedness; he thought the city was destined for judgment. After all, that is what they deserved. Weren't Sodom and Gomorrah destroyed because of their sin? This city deserved the same fate.

After running from God and experiencing the consequences of his actions, Jonah obeyed God, went to Nineveh, and preached. Their sin was so great that he didn't want them to turn from it; he wanted them to pay for it. That's why he ran in the first place. He knew God was a forgiving God, and Jonah felt these people didn't deserve forgiveness. When he finally went to Nineveh, Jonah thought he would preach judgment on the city, they would continue in their sin, and then he would sit back and watch it be destroyed. Then he could say that he was obedient, but they got what they deserved.

Just the opposite happened. Jonah walked throughout the city, urging people to turn from their wicked ways and proclaimed God's judgment if they didn't. In Jonah 3:5-9 the people respond by announcing a fast; the king decreed that everyone participate in the fast, wearing sackcloth. They believed in God and repented of their sin. They feared God and made a public declaration of penitence before Him. This was not what Jonah wanted. He wanted them to pay for the wickedness they had been involved in for so long. All he wanted was to preach this message, get out of the city, and watch God destroy them because of their wickedness. When that didn't happen, Jonah was angry.

Jonah said to God: "Isn't this what I said, Lord, when I was still at home? That is what I tried to forestall by fleeing to Tarshish. I knew that you are a gracious and compassionate God, slow to anger and abounding in love, a God who relents from sending calamity. Now, Lord, take away my life, for it is better for me to die than to live." (Jonah 4:2-3).

Because he didn't get what he wanted, Jonah threw a tantrum. He had expectations for how God should have acted against Nineveh, but God did not act according to that supposition. Jonah was upset that God didn't perform the way he thought He should, but God gave Jonah the space to voice his complaint. God allowed Jonah to say, "Things didn't turn out the way I thought they should." What's ironic is that Jonah told God that he knew He was gracious, compassionate, slow to anger, and abounding in love. Yet, he somehow wanted God to act differently.

Elijah's Struggle

Look also at Elijah's moment of disappointment. In 1 Kings 18, God worked through Elijah to miraculously show that Baal was a false god and that there was only one true God. The people who saw God bring fire down from heaven to consume Elijah's burnt offering fell on their faces and acknowledged the Lord as sovereign. What a great victory for Elijah! The prophets of Baal were defeated, and people turned to the Lord.

So why in 1 Kings 19:4 is he sitting under a tree, asking God to let him die? In verse 10, Elijah said, "I have been very jealous for the Lord , the God of hosts. For the people of Israel have forsaken your covenant, thrown down your altars, and killed your prophets with the sword, and I, even I only, am left, and they seek my life, to take it away."

In chapter 19's opening, when Jezebel heard about what Elijah had done to the Baal prophets, she sent him a message that she would make sure his fate was the same as theirs. Elijah thought, *Wait a minute. I've spent my whole life working for the Lord, showing people His power. He just performed a massive miracle through me, and this is my payment? Enough. This isn't how it's supposed to be. This isn't turning out the way I thought it would.* After this time of grief and disappointment, God did show Himself to Elijah. He didn't leave him in that place of questioning, but He did allow Elijah to go through the grief and confusion process. He allowed him to say, "This is not what I expected."

Jesus Allows You To Process Your Pain

Jonah, Elijah, and the men on the road to Emmaus forgot that God's ways are always better. Often, we forget this as well. In the middle of our grief, this truth is hard to understand. When our world comes crashing down unexpectedly and our future seems hopeless, seeing that God has bigger picture is not easy. We don't know how God can work when we mess it up and don't see a way to fix it. God has much more to give us, but we get blinded by the grief. And Jesus knows that. He so lovingly and patiently waits for us to see Him and all the beauty He brings out of our hopelessness. He allows us to say, "It didn't turn out the way I thought it should." He walks with us through the confusion and lets us voice our pain.

How badly we want to jump to the end of the story, to have all our tears wiped away and our hope fully restored. Because Jesus created and knows us perfectly, He knows we need time to process our experiences and cry out to Him. He will show us His beautiful will for us in His perfect timing, and in the meantime, we can tell Him, "I don't understand. Things didn't turn out the way I thought they should." He will listen and stay by our side the entire time. All of this is to teach us that we can trust Him. Remember that His purpose was worked out before the beginning of time. How foolish we are to think that our plans, hopes, and dreams could be better than His!

Take a moment to examine your grief. What are you grieving? What is it that you don't understand and makes you feel hopeless? Tell Jesus all of it. Tell Him that things didn't work out like you thought they should. Tell Him when you feel it's all your fault. He wants that for you. He wants you to go through all the stages it takes to process your tragedy. But He doesn't want you to stay there. As we look at the journey of the two men on the road to Emmaus, Jesus will reveal Himself, help you to understand, and open your eyes to the beauty after the heartbreak. Don't end your journey here. Keep walking down the road that the Lord has laid out for you. A glorious end to the sorrow is coming.

Journal Your Journey

First Kings 19:4 says, "[Elijah] came to a broom bush, sat down under it and prayed that he might die. 'I have had enough, Lord,'" he said. "Take my life; I am no better than my ancestors." Write out instances in which your life didn't turn out as you thought it would. For each one, take some time to think about how God worked the situation out for your good, even though it wasn't what you expected.

Maybe you're in a situation where things aren't what you thought they would be. Write a prayer asking God to show you how He works in your circumstances. Tell Him how you feel, and then sit and let Him speak to you.

Journey through the Book

1. Can you relate to Jonah? Have you had times when God's will for your life is not what you thought it would be?

2. What about Elijah? Can you relate to him? Have you ever had a great "mountaintop" experience with the Lord but felt defeated shortly afterward?

3. What kinds of things in your life now do you need to tell God, "I just don't understand. Why didn't this turn out differently?"

Journey through Scripture

Meditate on the following passages to keep your focus on Jesus:
- Jonah 4:10-11
- Psalm 34:18
- James 1:2-4

8

I've Heard But Can't Believe

In addition, some of our women amazed us. They went to the tomb early this morning but didn't find his body. They came and told us that they had seen a vision of angels, who said he was alive. Then some of our companions went to the tomb and found it just as the women had said, but they did not see Jesus (Luke 24:22-24).

After having downcast faces and admitting they were down because things didn't turn out as they thought they should, the men on the road to Emmaus told more of the story. They said to Jesus (although they still didn't know it was Him) that the women said He was alive. They described being amazed.

It couldn't be true, could it? Our companions went to the tomb, which was empty just like the women said . . . but they didn't see Jesus. We saw Him die, and we saw Him placed in a tomb. It's been three days. There is no way their story is true. We don't want to get our hopes up only to be disappointed again.

My Journey

I have felt this way myself. When I was stuck in my time of self-doubt, I still was able to grow in my relationship with the Lord. I learned His promises and believed increasingly in His faithfulness. I leaned on Him to help me when I felt down. I knew He would never leave me or forsake me. I believed with all my heart that my sins were forgiven. I read through the accounts of the Israelites and understood that I had the same God who would stand for me in times of trouble and hardship. It wasn't that I didn't have faith. My problem was that I wasn't living out His promises in that area of my life.

I had forgotten Romans 8:1: "Therefore, there is now no condemnation for those who are in Christ Jesus." I was allowing myself to be forgiven yet still held on to the thought that people would condemn me if they knew the truth about my past. I allowed Satan to dictate who I was in Christ instead of allowing Christ Himself to tell me. I knew God didn't condemn those who repent, but I didn't believe it was true for me, at least not for this particular sin. I couldn't put myself out there again to face the possibility of judgment and shame. I had heard this church family of mine say they didn't judge, but I couldn't believe it.

Doubting Thomas

We see this "I've heard it, but I can't believe it" played out in Thomas in John 20:24-25. Earlier in this chapter, Jesus appeared to Mary and then later to the other disciples. When He appeared to the other disciples, Thomas was not with them. So, they went and told Thomas with great excitement, "We have seen the Lord!"

At once, Thomas earned the title that would stick with him forever—Doubting Thomas. His response was, "Unless I see the nail marks in his hands and put my finger where the nails were, and put my hand into his side, I will not believe." Thomas didn't say that he doubted what his friends were telling him. He said he would not believe it until he saw it himself. In his grief over the loss he had just experienced, Thomas was not ready to have his heart broken again. The disciple had given his entire life to Jesus, and now that was all gone. He had no hope of receiving this fantastic news from his friends. He just could not believe it.

When we read this account, we quickly say, "Oh, Thomas, come on, just believe!" But that is because we know the story. We see through the pages of Scripture how this unfolded and how God's plan worked out. And we forget that Thomas and the other disciples were living the resurrection at the moment, unable to see the big picture.

How often do we react just like Thomas? We've heard Scripture and we know what is true, but we live as if we don't believe it. We can't see the big picture, so we can't imagine how our circumstances could possibly work out for good. Most of the time, we have our own idea of what the outcome should be. So, like in the last chapter, things don't turn out as we thought they would, and we allow ourselves to fall into unbelief. We allow Satan to slip into our thought lives and sneak lies into the middle of God's truth.

Don't Be Discouraged

Don't allow this to discourage you. When I think about all the times I have been a "Doubting Thomas," I am tempted to go on a guilt trip. How could I possibly call myself a believer and say that I trust Jesus and then so easily doubt His goodness to me? Remember that those thoughts are not from the Lord but from the devil. Satan wants nothing more than to discourage you and stunt your growth in the Lord. He wants you focused on your failures, forgetting that you already have victory through Jesus' death and resurrection. Don't allow Satan to steal your joy. You are in Christ and loved by Him no matter your circumstances.

Like the disciples and the men on the road to Emmaus, we live in the present. Unlike God, we cannot see the bigger picture. We don't understand how the past, present, and future all work together to create this beautiful and perfect purpose that He has laid out. We see the road full of potholes, and we can't see any way it can be smooth again. And when we are in times of deep grief or trouble, we have a tough time believing the good news that our fellow brothers and sisters in Christ share with us. We believe in God's promises but don't grasp them as if they are genuine in our lives.

Think back to the idea in chapter 2 of how important it is for us to meet with and talk to fellow believers to gain encouragement and support. God has given us this family to be bearers of good news in our times of sorrow and difficulty. The primary purpose of this family is to offer us encouragement. But like Thomas, it is in our times of most profound grief that we cannot receive this good news right away. We are too convinced that our hearts will be broken again. We need to see tangible evidence of God at work to help restore the hope that is in us. We need Jesus to step in and reveal Himself, or at least get a glimpse of something tangible we know He has done.

These are the times we need to ensure we are not neglecting meeting with our family in Christ. Look again at Thomas. Even though he was in the deepest grief of his life and was going through a roller-coaster of emotions, he still got together with the other disciples. He could have, as is our natural human tendency, gone off by himself and tried to figure all of this out on his own. Instead, he chose the companionship of his fellow believers. He went to them for the support of those who were grieving with him. What a blessing he received for making that choice! Had he stayed away, he would have missed seeing the risen Savior. He would have missed the chance to have his faith and joy restored.

You May Have To Wait

Don't miss the first few words of John 20:26: "A week later." A whole week passed between the disciples seeing Jesus and Thomas having the chance to see Him. An entire week for Thomas to wonder, think, hope, rationalize, and desire to believe. I'm sure that during that week, the disciples still gathered and talked about seeing the risen Lord. How could they not talk about it? So, for a full week, Thomas had heard about the resurrection but had not seen Jesus himself. A week can feel like an eternity when you are depressed and uncertain. The more days passed, it was probably harder for Thomas to believe what his companions were saying. The more time passed, the deeper the grief and hurt he felt in his heart that it was over. His teacher, his Lord, was gone.

Thomas heard what the rest of the disciples claimed they saw. He saw their excitement, but his hurt went too deep to believe it for himself. We can find ourselves in the same situation. Experiencing loss, hurt, and disappointment causes us to reach out to our fellow believers for support. Our wonderful Christian family supports and encourages us by reminding us of God's promises. Still, our hurt is too fresh and too deep to receive what they have to say. We say, "If I don't see God work for myself, I won't believe it." It's not a state in which we want to dwell. It's not a state we enjoy, but we get stuck there.

Another pothole along the road snags us during our journey. Just like the other potholes, the love of Christ won't leave us stuck there. Yes, Thomas had to wait a week, but then he got to experience the risen Jesus for himself. I can't answer why Jesus didn't show Himself to Thomas sooner, but I know this: Thomas finally believed. Even though we tend to be hard on doubting Thomas, his story lives on to give us the encouragement we need when we fall into the same unbelief. Jesus still lovingly showed Himself to Thomas, even though the disciple would not believe until he saw the Lord. If none of this happened, we wouldn't get the encouragement from verse 29. Today, we are blessed because we have not seen yet believe.

Jesus did not leave Thomas in his state of unbelief; as we will see, He did not leave the men on the road to Emmaus in their unbelief. He will certainly not abandon us on our dusty road either. We can trust Him to step in at just the right time and show Himself to us in a unique way that will renew our belief in Him. He won't be angry, just gentle and loving. So, like the man in Mark 9:24, we ask of Jesus, "Help me overcome my unbelief!" He will do just that, and we will be amazed at His goodness. As we continue to travel down the road with Him, He will teach us so much more!

JOURNAL YOUR JOURNEY

Think about Mark 9:24: "Immediately the boy's father exclaimed, 'I do believe; help me overcome my unbelief!'" Write about situations in your life where you are having a challenging time believing what God has said. Take some time to think about each one and why you are struggling with that promise.

Write a prayer asking God to show you areas where you are not living out His promises. Ask Him to help you overcome your unbelief

JOURNEY THROUGH THE BOOK

1. What is the importance of grasping God's Word not as factual but true for you?

2. Because we live in the present and cannot see the future as God can, we tend to have a narrow focus and only look at the problem. How can we avoid this and gain a more eternal perspective?

3. Why was continuing to meet with the other disciples important for Thomas? Why is maintaining meetings with our Christian family so meaningful for us?

JOURNEY THROUGH SCRIPTURE

Meditate on the following passages to keep your focus on Jesus:
- Romans 8:1
- John 20:29
- Mark 9:24

9

You Missed the Point

He said to them, "How foolish you are, and how slow to believe all that the prophets have spoken! Did not the Messiah have to suffer these things and then enter his glory?" (Luke 24:25-26).

Reading this part of the story of the men on the road to Emmaus, I can imagine Jesus, even with all the perfect patience He has, thinking, *Didn't you pay attention in school? You grew up studying the prophets, and you still don't get it!*

Jesus didn't say those words out of impatience. He only acts out of love. Jesus spoke this way to grab the men's attention, to make them open their eyes and understand that things had to be this way for God's perfect plan of salvation to work out. He wanted them to remember all they had studied and learned for years, all the prophecies that foretold the events they had just experienced. He wanted them to stop in their tracks and realize they were only looking at their circumstances in the present, not what they had been taught and what they knew was the truth.

My Journey

This moment for me came the first time I heard what is now my favorite song, "Redeemed" by Big Daddy Weave. That song tells the story of my life. I cling to its words when those old feelings of shame come crashing back. The first time I heard this song, I had a "how foolish you are" realization. The lyrics spoke to me as no other song had before, and I realized how much I was letting my past and struggle weigh me down.

I was living with the ghosts in my past that Big Daddy Weave sang about, and I was bound by my past failures. The part of the song that stuck out to me then and still speaks to me today is when the song says to stop fighting a battle that's already been won by Jesus. That line hit me like a ton of bricks. That's what I had been doing. I had been fighting a battle with my sin that Jesus had won when He rose from the dead. He has defeated Satan, and no amount of beating myself up would make me any more worthy of Him. I didn't even have a battle to fight; it had already been fought for me, so what was I doing? I am redeemed!

"How Foolish You Are"

Let's break down the key verses for this chapter and look at how they apply to us today. First, Jesus said, "How foolish you are . . ." Ouch. But think about it. We do the same things that the men on the road to Emmaus did. We stay focused on the pit we fell in, get discouraged, and complain about life not turning out as we thought it should. Then we allow ourselves to live in a state of unbelief. How foolish we can be!

Many of us have spent much time learning through devotional studies, Sunday school lessons, and sermons. After proclaiming that God is in control and declaring His plans are better, we still fall short when our world comes crashing down. We are foolish enough to believe the lies of Satan over the truth of God and whine about our circumstances. Even though we know that Jesus has a better plan than we do, we can easily fall into this trap of foolishness.

Jesus did not speak these words as condemnation, though. Instead of putting a guilt trip on them, He wanted to help them see that they knew better. Everything they had been taught about God could be trusted as true, but they weren't seeing it. We are the same way. We tend to have laser focus, only seeing the problem in front of us and not looking for God's truth in the situation. We know His Word, but in the moment, we're letting our circumstances cloud what we know about His character.

God knows and understands this about us. That is why He lovingly reminds us that we know better. The Lord wants us to take a deep breath and remember all we know about His love and promises. He wants us to get into the Word and read and reread all He says about Himself so we can escape that place of doubt.

We are in good company on this part of the road. So many times, Jesus had to stop His disciples and similarly talk to them. He used a common phrase with the disciples: "you of little faith." He meant the same thing as, "How foolish you are." Here are just a few examples (with my paraphrasing):

- Matthew 6:25-34 – If God feeds the birds and clothes the grass of the field, won't He also provide your needs, you of little faith?

- Matthew 8:23-26 – God is in control of nature, so what are you afraid of, you of little faith?

- Matthew 14:22-33 – You can do amazing things through Jesus' power, so why do you take your eyes off Him, you of little faith?

- Matthew 16:5-12 – God is trying to warn you about following the wrong people, so why don't you understand, you of little faith?

Do you hear the theme? How foolish we can be! We are prone to focus on the problem or pain we are experiencing and forget that God is sovereign and will never let us down. We need Jesus to say to us, "How foolish you are!" or "You of little faith!" We sometimes need to hear this put bluntly to snap us out of our wrong way of thinking.

As difficult as they are to hear, these phrases are the tow truck when all we see is the pothole. These words can be just what we need in those moments when the devil has a grip on our thoughts. We must follow two essential teachings in Scripture during these times. First, 2 Corinthians 10:5 says, "We demolish arguments and every pretension that sets itself up against the knowledge of God, and we take captive every thought to make it obedient to Christ." Secondly, Hebrews 12:1-2 says: "Throw off everything that hinders and run this race of life, keeping your eyes fixed on Jesus, not your worldly problems."

"How Slow To Believe"

Our focus verse for this chapter also conveys to us "how slow to believe." This concept is tough to admit because we know that we do believe. Most of us can stand and boldly proclaim that we believe Christ died for our sins, rose from the dead, and is coming back someday. We believe in God's unchanging nature and that He keeps His promises. We believe God works all things together for the good of those who love Him (Romans 8:28).

We don't see ourselves as unbelievers. However, when our faces are downcast in those moments of disappointment or grief, our knowledge of the truth can fade into the background if we're not careful. We put what we know on the back burner and live out our emotions instead of our faith. We don't take what we know as true and live it out. How slow we are to believe!

Finally, the last part of the passage from Luke 24 says, "Did not the Messiah have to suffer these things and then enter his glory?" I believe he meant, "Don't you see that it had to happen this way?" God has known His perfect will for the whole world from before time began. Before He created the universe, He knew who you would be, when you would be born, and the people you would know and love. God knew the career path you would take and when you would fail. He knew when you would lose loved ones, when you would succeed, and how you would get to every point in your life. All those seasons are part of a grand design by the Master Builder to draw us closer to Him. So yes, it's all for a purpose, one bigger than we'll ever know, and one we will see clearly when we stand face-to-face with Him.

We Won't Always Understand

When it comes right down to it, we really don't get it. That's one of the greatest mysteries of knowing Christ. We're not supposed to understand, at least not all of it. God has orchestrated this universe to work according to His perfect purpose, and He uses the good and the bad in our lives to ensure His perfect will for us. He also uses our lives to fulfill His even more significant purpose for the world. Here we are, messing it up all the time, yet God can still use every minute and every detail.

We can't possibly understand all that happens to us and why it happens. It's a blessing that we can't explain it. If we had perfect discernment of every situation, we would not need to trust God. He has designed us not to always get it. Consider what an honor it is to be part of the will of God. God, who doesn't need any of us, chooses to use us to accomplish His purposes. All He needs to do is speak and His will would be fulfilled, but He wants us to be a part of it. I can conceive of no greater honor.

Think about how much the disciples didn't understand, yet God still used them. In Luke 22:39-46, the disciples did not fully grasp what was about to happen. Jesus had just told them at dinner that His time was near, and the fulfillment of Scripture would be played out in Him. When they went to the garden of Gethsemane, He told them to pray so they would not fall into temptation. Yet what did they do? They fell asleep. They did not fully comprehend what was about to happen. Jesus often went off by Himself to pray, so for the disciples, this was another one of those times—just an ordinary night. They didn't understand. That was probably good. Had they fully grasped all that was going to happen, it may have been too overwhelming. Their hearts and minds may not have been able to handle knowing what they were about to experience.

The same could be said about us. Suppose we understood our circumstances and grasped the magnitude of what's happening today and tomorrow. In that case, it might be too much for us. God knows that, so He allows us to have limited understanding in some areas. Sometimes, we're just not meant to understand.

What We Can Understand

God does want us to know a few things, however. He wants us to understand that we can fully and completely trust Him with every detail of our lives. God wants us to know that He is sovereign in all things and has a future for us that is better than we could ever imagine. He wants us to know that we can go to Him with our doubts, fears, lack of understanding, or lack of faith, and He will respond only in love, not anger. He wants us to understand that the big picture is always that His resurrection gave us eternal life; everything else is meaningless.

So don't hear "You really don't get it" as words of condemnation. Hear them as words spoken in love from a Savior who understands that you will not always comprehend your circumstances. Don't hear "You of little faith" as a phrase to make you feel guilty. Hear it pointing you toward your Lord, who wants you to get one step closer to developing and following a firm faith. Take comfort that God has everything under His control, and it's okay to not get it. Then continue your journey down this road, always keeping your eyes fixed on Jesus. Stay on the walk and wait to see the glory that the Lord has in store!

Journal Your Journey

Read Matthew 6:25-34 on the next page. Make a list of everything you worry about. Then put those in the context of this passage and write why you have no reason to be anxious.

Write a prayer of confession to God about all the ways you worry about instead of relying on Him. Ask for His forgiveness and then thank Him for all the ways He provides for you every day.

Journey through the Book

1. Why would Jesus use such harsh words as foolish and slow to believe?

2. Was there a time in your life when you were foolish? Was there a time when you acted like the men on the road to Emmaus, and Jesus had to point out that you were not relying on Him the way you should?

3. Reread the passages where Jesus told His disciples, "You of little faith" (page 70). Can you relate to how the disciples felt when Jesus said those words?

Journey through Scripture

Meditate on the following passages to keep your focus on Jesus:

- Matthew 8:23-26
- 2 Corinthians 10:5
- Hebrews 12:1-2

Matthew 6:25-34

Therefore I tell you, do not worry about your life, what you will eat or drink; or about your body, what you will wear. Is not life more than food, and the body more than clothes? Look at the birds of the air; they do not sow or reap or store away in barns, and yet your heavenly Father feeds them. Are you not much more valuable than they? Can any one of you by worrying add a single hour to your life? And why do you worry about clothes? See how the flowers of the field grow. They do not labor or spin. Yet I tell you that not even Solomon in all his splendor was dressed like one of these. If that is how God clothes the grass of the field, which is here today and tomorrow is thrown into the fire, will he not much more clothe you—you of little faith? So do not worry, saying, "What shall we eat?" or "What shall we drink?" or "What shall we wear?" For the pagans run after all these things, and your heavenly Father knows that you need them. But seek first his kingdom and his righteousness, and all these things will be given to you as well. Therefore do not worry about tomorrow, for tomorrow will worry about itself. Each day has enough trouble of its own.

10

Rely on Scripture

*And beginning with Moses and all the Prophets, he explained
to them what was said in all the Scriptures concerning himself*
(Luke 24:27).

While Jesus allows us time to process and voice our grief
and confusion, what is beautiful about His love is that He
doesn't leave us there. When it's time to pull us out of our
human way of thinking, to haul us out of the places we are
stuck, He always points us back to the truth of Scripture.

Our human minds are so corrupt and capable of taking us
down so many rabbit holes of lies, and Scripture is the only
thing that can get us back into the right way of thinking. It's
almost as if we're walking this road in the dark, tripping into
holes and stumbling into mud puddles, and then Jesus hands
us a flashlight. We can suddenly see the road clearly, we don't
have to be afraid, and we can avoid the potholes.

If you've ever used a flashlight in the dark, you know that
it helps you to see in front of you, but everything off to the
side is still dark. The flashlight of Scripture works like this; it
lights the road in front of us and shows us the path clearly. We
should not look off the course to see what is in the darkness.

After Moses had given the Ten Commandments to the

Israelites, he told them, "So be careful to do what the Lord your God has commanded you; do not turn aside to the right or to the left" (Deuteronomy 5:32). Psalm 119:105 says, "Your word is a lamp for my feet, a light on my path." Use this flashlight of Scripture to keep you on the right path and out of the dangers found in the darkness.

My Journey

In my own walk, I have learned that reading the Word daily is one of the most important things I need to do. Even though I now have confidence that I am redeemed and don't have to live in the guilt and shame of my past, those insecure feelings still try to affect me.

Especially when I meet someone new who doesn't know my story, those thoughts of *What are they going to think of me?* can sneak its way back into my mind. Now that the Lord has met me in that insecurity, I can rely on His Word and character to tell me who I am. I hold on to verses like the following to keep my thoughts in line with God's:

- Romans 1:7 – I have redemption and forgiveness through the blood of Christ.
- 1 Peter 2:9 – I am chosen and holy in His sight; I am His special possession.
- John 15:15 – God calls me His friend.
- Romans 8:37 – I am victorious because He is victorious.
- 2 Corinthians 5:17 – I am a new creation; the old is gone, the new has come!

I could include so many more passages, but the point is to read and study the Word of God and rely on what He says about you—not what Satan wants you to believe about yourself and your situation. Your identity is in Christ alone, not in what others think of you, not what Satan says about you, and not what your past makes you out to be. You are a child of the living God!

The Pivotal Moment

Right here was the turning point for the men on the road to Emmaus. Jesus had allowed them to express their feelings. He had given them space to say things like, "Don't you get it?" and "Things didn't turn out the way I thought they should." He had answered with, "How foolish you are. Didn't it have to happen this way?" And now Jesus opened the Scriptures to them, reminding them of everything they had learned about the Messiah. He revealed what they knew in their heads but hadn't grasped with their hearts. Jesus showed them how far their human minds had strayed from the truth of His Word.

We go down a dangerous road when we allow our emotions to take over our thoughts. That's what these men had done. The men were so focused on an earthly Savior who would save Israel from the Roman rule that they had forgotten to go back and look at the Word of God they had been taught since they were boys. In those days, the primary education they received was from the Scriptures.

Remember, of course, that they only had the Old Testament. The New Testament was being played out in their very lives. They had been raised on Moses and the prophets. They knew the history of Israel and the signs that pointed to a coming Messiah. Jesus had been among them, and they missed Him! They knew the Scriptures and the prophecies but were not living as if they believed them. So, Jesus reminded them.

Don't we do the same? Many of us have several verses of the Bible memorized; perhaps we've studied Scripture for many years. We faithfully attend Sunday school, Bible study, and church services. It isn't that we don't know and believe the Scriptures, but we live as though they aren't true for us. When an issue arises, we try to find our own solutions rather than go to the One who holds the answers. However, when we take our problems to prayer, Jesus will open the Scriptures for us. He will lead us to passages we may have forgotten about and will give us the wisdom we need. He will point us back to the Word and all His promises.

The Importance of Scripture in the Early Church

Let's look at a group that had this same issue. In Acts 1:1-8, the disciples were gathered around the risen Jesus. He told them they would soon receive the indwelling of the Holy Spirit. But how did they respond? "Lord, are you at this time going to restore the kingdom to Israel?" They said the same thing that caused the men on the road to Emmaus to have downcast faces.

Not seeing the big picture, they didn't grasp the enormity of what Jesus had told them about the Holy Spirit and the power that would come with His indwelling. They were still focused on the earthly kingdom. Don't be too hard on them because we do this too. Jesus repeated His message and said, "But you will receive power when the Holy Spirit comes on you; and you will be my witnesses in Jerusalem, and in all Judea and Samaria, and to the ends of the earth." Then Jesus was taken up into heaven.

Just after this, when the disciples returned to Jerusalem, they finally started to understand. In Acts 1:12-26, the Holy

Spirit hadn't come yet, but they joined together in prayer. They weren't quite sure what was coming next, so they prayed. Then they relied on Scripture.

We see that Peter stood up and explained how Scripture was fulfilled by what happened to Judas Iscariot. He showed wisdom by applying that Scripture to how they should move forward. Then in Acts 2, when the Holy Spirit came upon them, Peter addressed the crowd with even more Scripture, and the power he had gained was obvious. Peter and the other disciples had finally realized that we can totally and completely rely on Scripture for truth and guidance.

The Danger of Doubting the Word

Life can be difficult when we rely on our human wisdom instead of God's. Look at the story of Adam and Eve in Genesis 3. They walked with God in a perfect garden created by the Lord. Remember that this was a perfect relationship; sin had not separated them from God yet. They were given His Word directly; He spoke right to them. He told them they could eat of any tree but one—the tree of the knowledge of good and evil. But Satan came along and tricked Eve into doubting God's Word.

We can blame Satan all we want, and he is very deceptive, but it was ultimately Eve's choice whether to eat that fruit. Don't miss this: Satan created the temptation, but Eve made the decision. She turned from what God had said and started to use her own human wisdom to justify what she was about to do. Genesis 3:6 says, "When the woman saw that the fruit of the tree was good for food and pleasing to the eye, and also desirable for gaining wisdom, she took some and ate it."

Here is what I see Eve did, and as much as I hate to admit

it, probably what I would have done as well. First, she said to herself, "Boy, that fruit does look good—the best in the whole garden. I can't see why God would withhold that from us." She began to talk herself out of God's words and into what she wanted.

Then the bigger danger came—she justified her actions. "I could be so wise if I ate that fruit. I could gain wisdom like God, then I could understand Him better. Wouldn't He want that for me?" So, she ate. Then she gave some to Adam, and he ate too. Again, we can blame Satan for Eve eating the fruit, and we can blame Eve for Adam eating the fruit, but really, whose fault was it? Adam and Eve knew God's words and took the fruit anyway. Why? Because they turned from the Word and started thinking with their human wisdom. They allowed Satan into their thought life.

So often, we find ourselves in the same place. We know what God's Word says is good for us. When going through challenging times, we know the promises of God and can rely on His Word. However, in adversity, sometimes we don't live what we know to be true. We start thinking and rationalizing for ourselves. Like the men on the road to Emmaus, we are too focused on the situation and lose sight of what God has so plainly said in Scripture. Like the men on the road, we need Jesus to get our focus back where it belongs. He will open the Word and explain its meaning, but we must be attentive to what He has to say.

Get into the Word

What I find interesting in this part of the road to Emmaus is that Jesus explained what the Scripture said concerning Himself, yet these two men still didn't know this stranger was

Jesus. They had to be amazed that this man had so much wisdom about the Scriptures. Their hearts burned within them while Jesus talked.

When you are confused, grieving, or just at a low point in your life, no places are better to turn to than the Word of God and prayer. Jesus will show you many amazing truths in the Scriptures if you are willing to let Him walk beside you and talk to you. Be sure you read the Word regularly to recognize His voice.

Avoid the potholes of the last chapter; don't stay in a place where Jesus says, "How foolish you are, and how slow to believe." Don't allow yourself to be the person Jesus tells, "You really don't get it." Instead, get out of your own head, stop relying on your wisdom, and allow Jesus to speak through His Word. Remember John 1:1 says that Jesus is the Word. Our walk becomes much less painful and more beautiful when Jesus steps in and reveals His truth to our hearts. Like the men on the road to Emmaus, allow Him to walk with you. Trust Him to listen to your pain. Open your ears to hear the Word He has to give you. Then bask in the love that only He can provide.

Stay on the road with me for a bit longer. Jesus has so much more to teach us through the journey of the two men on the road to Emmaus.

JOURNAL YOUR JOURNEY

Deuteronomy 5:32 says, "So be careful to do what the Lord your God has commanded you; do not turn aside to the right or to the left." Write out some ways that you tend to look to the right or to the left instead of focusing on what Scripture has laid out in front of you. Commit to looking to the Word first for answers instead of relying on your wisdom.

Write a prayer asking God to convict you in areas where you rely on yourself instead of Him. Ask Him to guide you with His truth.

JOURNEY THROUGH THE BOOK

1. Think about Scripture as the "flashlight" of life. In what ways does it guide you? How does it keep you out of dark places?

2. What is the danger of relying on our emotions rather than the Word of God?

3. What lessons can you apply to your own life by studying what Adam and Eve experienced?

JOURNEY THROUGH SCRIPTURE

Meditate on the following passages to keep your focus on Jesus:

- Deuteronomy 5:32
- 1 Peter 2:9
- Romans 8:37

11

Invite Him In

As they approached the village to which they were going, Jesus continued on as if he were going farther. But they urged him strongly, "Stay with us, for it is nearly evening; the day is almost over." So he went in to stay with them (Luke 24:28-29).

One of the most meaningful customs in Jesus' day was hospitality. In that culture, if someone needed a place to stay and the evening was approaching, it was common to invite that individual to stay the night, even if that person was a total stranger. This practice is foreign to us in modern American culture. We tend to shy away from strangers and aren't comfortable inviting them into our homes.

Our culture is different from the one in Jesus' day. Inviting Jesus in was one of the most essential steps the men on the road to Emmaus took. If they had neglected to do so, they would have missed the best part of the journey—the moment their eyes were opened.

Inviting Jesus into our lives is the single most crucial decision we will ever make. Without it, we would miss the greatest blessing of all—the salvation of our souls. When we practice hospitality with Jesus, we receive His Holy Spirit. Even beyond the miracle of salvation, we also receive power, peace, and victory.

So, we don't just invite Him in once. We invite Him for the first time to gain salvation, then we ask daily for the refreshing of His Spirit so we can have the abundant life He promised. Moment by moment, we decide to allow Him into our circumstances, to trust that He knows what is best for us. When we do so, we live in the knowledge that He holds our situation in His hands and will work all out for our good. Daily we invite Him to come in and be Lord of every aspect of our lives.

My Journey

I had to learn this lesson through my struggle with shame, guilt, and insecurity. After rededicating my life to Christ, I knew He lived inside of me and would never leave me. I didn't realize how powerful it is to keep inviting Him in every day, every moment. Until I learned this, I would go back and forth in my struggle.

I would feel more secure in Christ, and then the old feelings of shame would wash over me again. The knowledge of the Holy Spirit's presence was there, but I wasn't grasping the power that He could have in my life. Finally, I realized I could not take the Holy Spirit's presence for granted. I had to intentionally invite Him to take over my thoughts and leave my situation in His hands.

Invite Him in and Make Him Lord

Practicing hospitality with Jesus is not a one-and-done event. Inviting Him into every day, every moment is critical. When we don't, we start to make decisions and figure things out based on our understanding. That is a dangerous road to travel. Remember the flashlight of Scripture from the last chapter?

Now we add the Holy Spirit, who is like the GPS of our souls, warning us when we are about to take a wrong turn. We all know that the GPS in our cars does no good if we don't turn it on or ignore it. The same concept pertains to the Holy Spirit. If we don't invite Him into the moment or choose to ignore His leading, we will head down the wrong road no matter how many times He gives the "reroute" warning.

Not only do we invite Him in, but we make room for Him to stay. Consider the Shunammite woman in 2 Kings 4:8-10. The only way to hear from God in her day was through the prophets. Elisha the prophet would often come to her house for a meal when he was in the area. The woman recognized that he was a man of God and held the very words of God, so in verse 10, she decided she should make room for him to stay in when he came to visit. This room contained three everyday items that have special meaning for us today: a bed, a lamp, and a chair. For Elisha, it gave him a place during his travels to rest, a light to read and write by, and a chair in which to sit comfortably. For us, there is so much more.

When we invite God into the room we have prepared for Him in our lives, these three ordinary items turn into great blessings for ourselves and others. When Jesus takes up residence within us, He gives us perfect peace and rest like a comfortable bed. The rest we have in Jesus is like no other, a peaceful way in our lives that is beyond comprehension and explanation. Philippians 4:7 describes this as "the peace of God, which transcends all understanding."

His presence in us is also a light for all to see—a lamp that is always kept burning. Others can see that light in us, and it can dispel the darkness of this world. Matthew 5:14 describes it this way: "You are the light of the world. A town built on a hill cannot be hidden."

The last item, maybe the most important, is a chair. In the original language, the word used for the chair was throne. Jesus needs to be enthroned in our lives. We need to allow Him to be set up as Lord and King over who we are and all we do. First Peter 3:15 says, "But in your hearts revere Christ as Lord." When He is given that proper place in our lives, the rest and light become even more apparent. So, invite Him in and give Him a place to stay.

Open the Door

Jesus is waiting and longing to be invited into your life. He says in Revelation 3:20, "Here I am! I stand at the door and knock. If anyone hears my voice and opens the door, I will come in and eat with that person, and they with me." Picture that in your own life. Jesus is standing at the door, knocking, waiting for you to answer. He won't force His way in; He will patiently wait.

I sometimes think as believers, we read this verse as if it is addressed to unbelievers, to those who need to open their hearts to the salvation message. It is undoubtedly effective to use in that circumstance. But look at who Revelation 3 addresses: the church in Laodicea. This was written to believers, people who knew the living Savior but were not tapping into the power that belonged to them through the Holy Spirit.

That means that even those who have accepted Jesus as their Savior still need to open that door. In our struggles, confusion, and grief, we often look around our own lives for answers and don't answer the door. We look to other people, helpful books, read the Bible, and even go to prayer—all good and necessary behavior. But even in our prayers, we forget the one crucial action we need to take—asking Jesus to step into the situation.

We don't just need Him to show up; we need Him to take over. Instead of asking Him to help and looking for answers in Scripture, we need to ask Him to *completely* take over. We need to put the situation into His hands and let go of it ourselves. Give Him the power to work in the circumstance. It is way too easy for us to forget or live in disbelief of the power we have when Jesus takes up residence in our lives.

The Holy Spirit's Power

Look in Acts 2 at the apostles' power when they received the Holy Spirit. They all started speaking in languages they didn't know, and people from all different cultures could hear them declaring the wonders of God. Then Peter stood up and gave one of the most powerful sermons ever preached.

Out of fear, Peter had denied Jesus three times the night before He was crucified. But now Peter boldly preached, and about three thousand people were saved that day. That's power. We have that same power living in us but simply don't utilize it. Do you realize that it was the power of the Holy Spirit who raised Jesus from the dead? And His power lives in you! Don't ever let the enemy tell you otherwise.

Consider the following passages of Scripture about Jesus living in you, and allow them to challenge, teach, and encourage you as you walk along your road:

- 2 Corinthians 13:5 – Examine yourself to see if you have allowed Christ to take up residence in your heart. If you haven't, open the door and give Him what's rightfully His throne.

- Romans 8:10 – Even though you should be dead in your sin, you are alive because of Christ in you.

- 2 Corinthians 4:6-7 – Even though we live in these earthly bodies (these jars of clay), we have the light of Christ shining through us.

- Galatians 2:20 – Once you have invited Jesus in, you have shared in His crucifixion, and it is no longer you who lives, but Christ lives in you. You can now live your life by faith and not by sight.

- Ephesians 3:16-17 – Jesus will strengthen you with power and dwell (reside) in your heart.

What wonderful, powerful words these are! If we open that door and invite Him in, that power is ours.

Jesus Will Eat with You

Go back to Revelation 3:20. Not only will Jesus come in when you open the door, but He also says He will eat with you and you with Him. Why is that significant? First, consider what Jesus did when He revealed Himself to people after His Resurrection. In the case of the men on the road to Emmaus, He went in and ate with them. In Luke 24:41, He appeared to the disciples again after the incident with the men on the road to Emmaus. After revealing Himself, He asked, "Do you have anything to eat?" When He stood on the shore and revealed Himself to His disciples in John 21:12, He was making breakfast. When we get to heaven with Him, we will partake in the wedding feast of the Lamb.

The Lord knows that eating together is intimate and special. When we sit together over a meal, we can have deep conversations and fellowship with each other that is sweet and unique. We receive a blessing when we invite Jesus into our home, and He eats with us! The men on the road to Emmaus had no idea what they were in for when they asked this stranger to stay with them. They were simply being obedient to the custom of hospitality. But in doing so, they were about to receive a blessing like no other—the ability to finally recognize the risen Savior.

We have this excellent opportunity as well. Even in our most profound times of loss, our most painful places, our moments of confusion, and the deepest potholes of our lives, we have this opportunity to invite Jesus in. Remember, He is right there knocking; all it takes is us to open the door. When we do, He will not only enter but also sit down to eat with us, have an intimate conversation, and help us through our trials. He will show us how His power and grace are sufficient for anything we face. Imitate the men on the road to Emmaus and urge Him to enter. Don't miss the chance of the sweetest and most loving encounter you could ever experience.

Even though the men had reached the end of their walk on the road, the journey wasn't over. Jesus had so much to show them; He had a victory to give them that only He could provide. Keep traveling with me as we see how their story ends in excitement and triumph. Be encouraged that yours can be the same!

JOURNAL YOUR JOURNEY

Read Revelation 3:20: "Here I am! I stand at the door and knock. If anyone hears my voice and opens the door, I will come in and eat with that person, and they with me." Write about some areas in your life where you need to let Jesus in. Where is He knocking, and you haven't opened the door?

Write a prayer asking the Lord to enter the situations you described above. Ask Him to reveal to you when you are shutting Him out. Then take the time to sit quietly with Him and invite Him in.

JOURNEY THROUGH THE BOOK

1. What do we miss when we don't practice hospitality with Jesus—when we don't let Him into our lives?

2. Think about the account of the Shunammite woman in 2 Kings 4:8-10. Can you say you have provided the bed, the lamp, and the chair for the Lord in your life? Which area do you think you need to work on more?

3. What do you picture when you read about the Lord coming to eat with you and you with Him? What kinds of emotions does that stir up inside of you?

JOURNEY THROUGH SCRIPTURE

Meditate on the following passages to keep your focus on Jesus:
- Romans 8:10
- Ephesians 3:16-17
- Revelation 3:20

12

Your Daily Bread

When he was at the table with them, he took bread, gave thanks, broke it and began to give it to them (Luke 24:30).

After Jesus had been invited in by the men on the road to Emmaus, He broke bread and gave it to the men. This act was significant because *Jesus* broke the bread, not the men. According to the hospitality customs of the day, the hosts were to provide food, water, and shelter to their guests.

However, this was not a cultural slipup for the two men. Jesus' plan all along the road to Emmaus was to reveal Himself in such a compelling way that the men would be amazed and never forget the encounter. Jesus used bread in the most substantial part of their journey—another ordinary item that has extraordinary significance.

My Journey

In my own life, I have had times where I desperately needed to see God at work. I have never heard Him shout out from heaven in a loud voice in those moments. On the contrary, I see the small ways He works in everyday things. Maybe I hear a lyric from a song that just resonates with me in a way it never has before. Sometimes it is a familiar passage of Scripture I read that takes on a whole new meaning for me that day. Often, it is through journaling my prayers that He makes something clear to me. Or it can be as simple as seeing His beautiful power in a sunrise or sunset or a bird against the backdrop of a beautiful, blue sky. He has also spoken to me through a short, seemingly meaningless conversation with another believer. All those things show that He often chooses to reveal Himself to me in a small, simple gesture, like breaking bread. These seemingly unimportant tokens are all worthwhile. They are just the bread I need for that day to help me overcome my confusion, doubt, and insecurity.

Breaking Bread with Jesus

Jesus loves to break bread with His friends. He loves to have fellowship with us that is intimate and real. He wants to sit with us daily around a table and reveal Himself in a mighty way through simple signs and truths. Some are easy to miss. We need to get in tune with His Spirit so we don't miss the daily bread He offers us. Overlooking these small gestures is easiest when we are having trouble. Jesus will provide us with manna, daily bread, and the Bread of Life, but we need to sit down at the table with Him and receive it.

Let's remember what the men had experienced and what Jesus had just walked them through. First, in Jerusalem, they witnessed the brutal death of the One they thought was the Redeemer of Israel. They began their walk to Emmaus shortly afterward, feeling defeated and afraid of the future. A random man (or so they thought) joined them on their walk while they talked about all of this. After pouring out their hearts to this stranger, He started to explain everything to them from the Scriptures. After inviting Him in, they likely were anxious to hear what else He had to say. Instead of explaining further, He broke bread.

So much substance lies in this seemingly small act. First, before Jesus was crucified, Jesus also broke bread with His disciples when He wanted to tell them what would happen to Him. In Matthew 26:26, we see this memorable time that the disciples had with Jesus, the event that we call the Last Supper. While they were eating the Passover meal, Jesus "took bread, and when he had given thanks, he broke it and gave it to his disciples, saying, 'Take and eat; this is my body.'" Notice the parallel to what He said to the two men in our account. In Luke 24:30, "He took bread, gave thanks, broke it and began to give it to them."

When Jesus wanted to reveal a profound truth, He often used the breaking of bread. For His disciples at the Last Supper, it was to show them that He was about to become their perfect sacrifice, "the Lamb of God who takes away the sin of the world" (John 1:29). For the two men in Luke 24, it was to reveal to them that He indeed was the risen Savior. Scripture had been fulfilled, and their lives would never be the same.

Lesson Learned from Bread

This was not the first time Jesus had used bread to teach something about Himself. In John 6:25-40, much of the same crowd who was present when Jesus fed the five thousand had come looking for Him. These people had just witnessed a fantastic miracle. After a long day, this large crowd had just been fed with five small loaves and two fish. The next day, many of them had come to see what other miracles He might perform, but He had a much bigger lesson to teach them.

He explained that He was the Bread of Life and that anyone who comes to Him would never hunger again. He also said that the manna from heaven that fed the Israelites while wandering in the desert symbolized the One who would come from the Father and provide their daily bread. The people were so focused on physical bread and needs that many missed this vital teaching. Let's make sure we don't miss it.

In Exodus 16:4, God told Moses, "I will rain down bread from heaven for you. The people are to go out each day and gather enough for that day." The Israelites were not to worry about gathering enough for the future or storing the food to ensure they would have enough. They were to pick up only what they needed each day. As a lesson, those who gathered more found that the manna was full of maggots the next day. God was showing the Israelites that He would provide for their *daily* needs, that He would give them their daily bread, and that they could trust Him.

The people in Jesus' day knew this history. They knew all about how their ancestors survived in the desert by the divine hand of God. These people would have had this history handed down to them, which was an integral part of their education. When Jesus conversed with the crowd in John 6:32-35 about being the Bread of Life, He revealed that He would provide their daily bread. He demonstrates the same to us today.

Our Daily Bread

Let's look at the words Jesus gave His disciples when they asked Him to teach them to pray. We could talk about so much in that prayer pattern, but let's focus on this one phrase in Matthew 6:11: "Give us today our daily bread." The prayer that Jesus taught His disciples, which we refer to as the Lord's

Prayer, is one of the most memorized passages of Scripture, and rightfully so. It is the pattern that Jesus gave to us to pray to our heavenly Father. Too often, we learn the passage, recite it, and don't think about the true meaning of what we are praying. Too often, we ignore the strength behind the words.

When studying the Lord's Prayer, we often get to this part, saying that we are praying to God to provide for our daily needs. That is correct. We need to rely on God to give us what we need each day, and we need to ask Him for that. Right after providing this pattern of prayer, however, Jesus promised we wouldn't have to worry about these needs. Remember Matthew 6:25-34 from chapter 9. This is where Jesus says not to worry about our daily needs, like food and clothing. He used examples from nature like the birds of the air and the grass of the field. If God takes care of those, won't He also take care of you? I think Jesus is trying to show us that the provision of God is a given if we are His children. He will provide for us, and we don't have to worry about that, ever.

What if "Give us today our daily bread" means more than just "Please provide my daily needs?" What if, when we pray those words, we ask Jesus to come in and be our daily bread? Look again at Matthew 6:25: "Is not life more than food, and the body more than clothes?" You see, the only thing we need each day is Jesus. If we have Him, we already have everything we need. Jesus specifically says not to worry about His daily provision because He has already taken care of it. He instructs us in Matthew 6:33-34 that if we just seek God's kingdom and righteousness, everything we need will be given to us. God wants us to seek Him and Him alone. He wants us to realize that He is the manna from heaven, the only thing we need.

When we allow Him to be our daily bread, we open ourselves up to see Him revealed to us in ways that we would never have seen otherwise. We will see in the next chapter that the men on the road to Emmaus had their eyes opened marvelously after this breaking of bread. Don't miss the weight of this.

Let's put it all together. First, Jesus stands at the door of your heart and knocks. When you open that door, He will come in and eat with you. When Jesus breaks the bread, He will reveal to you that He is the Bread of Life, the only thing you need. He wants to do this in your life daily. He wants to be invited into every day, every situation, every moment.

Don't think of asking Him in as something you only need to do once. Remember, we are to ask for our daily bread. We need to open that door each and every day and let Him show us that He will take care of us today. We are to seek His kingdom and His righteousness. Seeking isn't something you do only once. It's a continual process, something you must commit to daily, even moment by moment. Remember this when you pray, "Give us today our daily bread." Don't allow that to be a shallow prayer of simply asking for the "stuff" you need. Ask for the Bread of Life to come in, reveal Himself to you, and be the only sustenance you need.

The men on the road to Emmaus were about to see just how amazing that revealing would be. They were about to see how something as small as breaking bread could be the one move that made all the difference. They were about to experience something extraordinary in a seemingly ordinary act. Stay on their journey and experience the joy they felt when they finally saw their risen Savior.

JOURNAL YOUR JOURNEY

Think about John 6:35: "Then Jesus declared, "I am the bread of life. Whoever comes to me will never go hungry, and whoever believes in me will never be thirsty." Write about how you have relied on God to provide for you but have neglected to allow Him to be your daily bread. Think of ways to remember to depend on Him for everything, not just your physical needs.

Write a prayer asking God to be the daily sustenance you need. Take time to give everything over to Him. Commit to do this daily.

JOURNEY THROUGH THE BOOK

1. What are some small, simple ways God has revealed Himself to you?

2. Think about the simple act of sitting down to a meal with friends. What is so special and intimate about this time together? How can we do the same with Jesus?

3. In Matthew 6, Jesus gave His pattern for prayer, and then He went on to teach us not to worry about our daily needs. How is "Give us today our daily bread" connected with "Do not worry"? In what ways do you need Jesus to be your daily bread today?

JOURNEY THROUGH SCRIPTURE

Meditate on the following passages to keep your focus on Jesus:
- Matthew 7:7
- John 6:32-35
- Matthew 26:26

13

You Finally See

Then their eyes were opened and they recognized him, and he disappeared from their sight (Luke 24:31).

Here is the moment that all the previous events were fore-shadowing. The two men on the road to Emmaus have their eyes opened and understand what happened in Jerusalem and what Jesus had taught them along the way. Their eyes were opened, and they recognized their risen Lord and Savior.

I can't imagine what went through their minds when they realized it was Jesus who walked the road with them. Scripture doesn't say this specifically, but I believe that the moment they recognized Jesus was when He handed them the bread. He held out His hands with bread to feed them, and there were the nail marks. He wasn't just giving them bread; He was opening their eyes to see Him.

My Journey

As I noted earlier, I experienced a similar moment when a pastoral couple shared a story like mine. When the wife of that couple approached me afterward and talked to me about it, my eyes were opened. I could see clearly for the first time that Jesus had taken all my guilt and shame, and I didn't have to live under it anymore. There was no reason to hide my past because it was part of my beautiful story of redemption.

Then, the first time I heard "Redeemed" by Big Daddy Weave, I had another eye-opening instant. I learned to stop struggling against something Jesus had already taken care of. Jesus had won the battle for me when He died on the cross and rose from the dead. When Jesus revealed Himself plainly to me, the world came into clear focus. It was like having my sight restored.

Healing Our Blindness

Several times throughout His earthly ministry, Jesus healed the blind. One example is the blind beggar in Jericho in Luke 18:35-43. As this man sat along the road, he cried out to Jesus to recover his sight, and Jesus said, "Your faith has made you well." In Matthew 9:27-30, two blind men followed Jesus down the road, crying for Him to have mercy on them and give them their sight. Jesus healed them, saying, "According to your faith be it done to you."

In the account in John 9, Jesus used a different method of healing. He made mud with His saliva, put it on the blind man's eyes, and told him to wash in the Pool of Siloam. When the man was questioned about receiving his sight and who healed him, he said one of the most well-known phrases in Scripture: "One thing I do know. I was blind but now I see!" (John 9:25)

Jesus wants us to see Him and seek Him. He wants to show Himself to us. Jesus knows the perfect timing and way to do that. With the men on the road to Emmaus, He had to let them go through their time of grieving and questioning. Jesus had to remind them of what they knew about Scripture and prophecy.

Then, when their hearts were ready, He revealed Himself to them. For those who were physically blind, Jesus wanted them to have faith that He could heal them, that He was able to restore their sight, and that He could do the impossible. In the case of the man who washed in the Pool of Siloam, Jesus wanted that healing to become a testimony of what God can do.

Jesus wants all of this for us as well. When we go through times of confusion, grieving, loss, and trouble, He wants us to allow Him to walk beside us. At the end of that walk, Jesus wants to reveal Himself in a mighty way by reaching out His hands with the bread we so desperately need and by revealing those nail marks. He wants us to know that we don't have to focus on the problems and trials in this life. His death and resurrection overcame the sin of the world.

Remember what He told us in John 16:33: "In this world you will have trouble. But take heart! I have overcome the world." He wants us to understand that, although trials and tribulations will come, He has overcome all of them. That doesn't mean we won't grieve and sometimes walk in confusion, but we don't have to stay there. Allow Jesus to hold out that Bread of Life to you and focus on the nail marks in His hands—the scars that show you have the victory in Christ.

Healing Requires Obedience

Go back to John 9 and examine the lesson Jesus taught when He healed the blind man in the Pool of Siloam. Notice that Jesus did not cure the man instantly but used this healing as a more powerful lesson. First, the disciples were trying to figure out why this man was born blind. Was it he or his parents who sinned? Jesus told them it was neither, but the blind man had been healed "so that the works of God might be displayed in him" (v. 3). You see, sometimes our struggles serve a larger purpose, a chance for God to show His power.

We see from the other blind men that Jesus could have instantly healed this man, but He didn't. Instead, He put mud on his eyes and told him to go and wash in the Pool of Siloam. Then Jesus let the man walk away. The man had to act out of faith and obey what Jesus asked him to do. When he did, his sight was restored. When the people saw that this man, who had been blind all his life, could see, they brought him before the Pharisees, so they could investigate the matter. After they questioned the man and listened to his testimony, he was thrown out by the Pharisees because they didn't want to believe in Jesus.

This Scripture of healing the blind man is like the walk the men on the road to Emmaus took; it is also much like our own. Jesus did not immediately remove the sadness and defeat the men on the road to Emmaus felt. He instead allowed them to voice their hurt. He also used their grief for a larger purpose— to give them a powerful testimony to share with others. The healing was a process, not an instant relief.

We sometimes must wait for our restoration as well. Jesus can heal instantly, but He doesn't always choose to work that way. Sometimes He wants to teach use more through our pain. Jesus will always enter the picture, but sometimes He remains quiet and unnoticed until our hearts are softened to hear His voice. Like the man at the Pool of Siloam, the men on the road to Emmaus had to act out of obedience. They had to be obedient to the custom of hospitality. Had they not been, they would have remained blind and mired in their grief and confusion because of their inability to recognize Jesus as the risen Savior. We too must walk in obedience.

When times are tough, and we don't feel like reading Scripture or praying, those are the times we must not neglect them. We also have a powerful testimony awaiting us, but we won't see it if we act out of a heart of disobedience. Like the blind man at the Pool of Siloam, we will likely run into those who don't want to hear or believe our testimony. We can't let that discourage us from being bold and saying, "I was blind, but now I see!"

The Bigger Lesson

Now let's think about Jesus' lesson taught through the healing of this man at the Pool of Siloam. Read John 9:35-41. Jesus heard that the Pharisees had thrown the man out, so He went to find him. Even though the religious leaders disbelieved the man healed of his blindness, he believed in Jesus and gained salvation. But then Jesus revealed the real lesson to be learned here: "For judgment I have come into this world, so that the blind will see and those who see will become blind" (v. 39).

All the years this man was allowed to remain blind led to this moment. His struggles were meant for a much bigger purpose. Jesus said these words in front of the Pharisees, who were very offended. He told the Pharisees that they couldn't claim to understand salvation and then continue to live in their sin. Once we have received the message of salvation, we can choose whether to remain in our sin or turn from it.

Jesus taught this same principle to His disciples when He explained to them that the world would hate them because of Him. In John 15:22-24, He said,

> *If I had not come and spoken to them, they would not be guilty of sin; but now they have no excuse for their sin. Whoever*

hates me hates my Father as well. If I had not done among them
the works no one else did, they would not be guilty of sin. As it
is, they have seen, and yet they have hated both me and my
Father.

What did Jesus mean? Once a person hears about the saving grace of Jesus Christ, there is no excuse. We get to choose whether to turn from our sin, and once we've heard, we have nobody to blame but ourselves if we continue our sinful lifestyle. Once Jesus restores our sight, and we can clearly see the path of salvation, we no longer have any excuse.

This is a hard lesson to receive. Many people want to think of Jesus as loving, gentle, and compassionate. Of course, He is all those things. But Jesus is also the righteous judge of the world. In John 9:39, He said, "For judgment I have come into this world." He was about to suffer on the cross in the ultimate act of love so humankind could receive the salvation that could only come through Him. Those who reject His sacrifice are under judgment. The only path to eternal life is through the One who took all sin upon Himself. Jesus conquered sin and death for good when He rose from the dead. When we believe in Him and turn from our sinful way of life, dying to ourselves, we live for Christ. That is how our spiritual blindness is healed.

While Jesus heals us spiritually and releases us from the bondage of sin, that is not the only healing we receive by believing in Him. We can also find redemption of our pain, sadness, grief, and confusion. The men on the road to Emmaus found redemption when Jesus handed them the bread. Suddenly, everything came into clear focus. The Scriptures Jesus had explained on the road made sense then, and they could see Jesus as their Savior. He was alive!

We can have this redemption as well. When we pour out

our hearts to Jesus and are honest with Him, He will make Himself known to us. He will open our eyes. He will never leave us alone in our suffering. He will teach us many things along the road that we couldn't possibly have understood without going through a time of confusion and pain.

Jesus Disappeared?

I find the last part of our focus verse for this chapter intriguing: "He disappeared from their sight." Does that mean He will reveal Himself and then leave us? Absolutely not. Remember the promise He made to never leave or forsake us. The men on the road to Emmaus had to come to terms with how wrong their thinking had been when they were walking with Jesus. They had to figure out what they would do with the knowledge that He was still alive. They had to act out of faith that their experience was real. I'm sure they had to get over the initial shock of seeing someone they thought to be dead right in front of them.

Unlike the men on the road to Emmaus, we are blessed with the Holy Spirit. Jesus lives within us. Since we do not have Jesus physically present with us, we fall under the category of those in John 20:29: "Blessed are those who have not seen and yet have believed." We are to adopt the attitude described in 2 Corinthians 5:6-10: "We live by faith and not by sight ... so we make it our goal to please him." When our eyes are opened to His grace and mercy, see the salvation of our souls, and the Holy Spirit comes upon us with power, we are blessed. We are amazed when Jesus reveals Himself to us in the middle of our grief and confusion. What He has been trying to teach us along the roads we walk will become apparent, and we will be in awe of the way God cares for us.

I hope this gives you the desire to want to live a life that pleases Him. I pray that, even during the tough times, you can see that Jesus has so much to lovingly teach you. Stay on the journey. As dusty as it may be, keep to the road. Jesus is waiting to show you something beyond your wildest imagination!

Journal Your Journey

John 16:33 says, "I have told you these things, so that in me you may have peace. In this world you will have trouble. But take heart! I have overcome the world." Write about how Jesus has helped you overcome. Thank Him that because He has overcome the world, you have too.

Maybe you have a situation in which you still feel defeated. Write a prayer asking God to help you overcome. Allow yourself to sit in His victory, even if you don't yet feel it.

Journey through the Book

1. Look at the three examples of Jesus healing the blind given in this chapter. How are they the same? What do you notice that is different?

2. How was Jesus revealing Himself to the men on the road to Emmaus like the blind being healed?

3. What was the bigger lesson that Jesus was trying to teach in John 9:35-41 and repeated in 15:22-24? How does this stir your heart towards obedience?

Journey through Scripture

Meditate on the following passages to keep your focus on Jesus:
- John 9:25
- John 16:33
- 2 Corinthians 5:6-10

14

The Burning within You

They asked each other, "Were not our hearts burning within us while he talked with us on the road and opened the Scriptures to us?" (Luke 24:32)

After Jesus disappeared from their sight, these men realized that they should have recognized Him much sooner than they did. While they walked along the road, Jesus explained to them, from Moses through the prophets, that what had taken place in Jerusalem had to happen to fulfill the Scriptures. Jesus spoke with authority, and as He did, the men's hearts burned within them.

The burning they felt is conviction. It's that gut feeling that something isn't right, that we need to change how we think. These men had this conviction as they walked with Jesus, but it wasn't until He revealed Himself that they understood the burning within them.

My Journey

I had a burning within me throughout my struggles with insecurity and shame. Many times I felt an urging in my spirit to share my story. I know now that the Holy Spirit was telling me that everything was okay. I could share my past with other believers, and what makes a testimony beautiful is the concept of "This is where I was but look where God has brought me." Unfortunately, I quenched that burning with my fear, shame, and insecurities. Hearing those women talk about me at the first church I went to significantly impacted my self-image more than I imagined.

I didn't see that part of my life as covered by the blood of Christ. I saw it as something to be ashamed of, something to hide. But God placed a burning within me to change my way of thinking. He showed me that we all have a story, and even the ugly parts—especially the ugly parts—are made beautiful by His sacrifice. However, like the men on the road to Emmaus, I had to walk down a long, dusty, pothole-filled road to understanding.

We Misunderstand

In their grief and sorrow, the men on the road to Emmaus couldn't recognize the voice of Jesus. Something inside of them knew. That burning within them was trying to make them understand what had happened. But their faces were downcast because they were in a deep pothole on their road, their thoughts were clouded, and they couldn't grasp the miracle right before them. In their grief, they misunderstood what Jesus was trying to teach them. It's easy for us to read this account and say, "Hello! Wake up, guys! This is Jesus talking to you!" Let's not be too hard on them until we examine our hearts.

We also experience this burning within us. The Holy Spirit always speaks into our lives, but our vision sometimes gets clouded. Sometimes, like these men, it is blurred because of our grief or confusion. Other times it is confused because we think we have the answers and solutions, and we miss the better answer only the Lord can provide. Sometimes we simply misunderstand the message the Lord sends us. Whatever the case, we put out the flame burning within us and go our own way. Yet Jesus still speaks. He still lovingly walks along the road with us, explaining everything to us through the person of His Holy Spirit. How much more blessed we would be if we fanned the flame instead of stifling it!

One person in Scripture who misunderstood the burning within him was Samuel. While he was a boy, Samuel ministered under Eli. One night as they lay sleeping, Samuel heard a voice call his name. So, he went to Eli and said, "Here I am; you called me." As his loving guardian, Eli said, "I did not call; go back and lie down" (1 Samuel 3:5). This happened two more times until finally, Eli realized God was calling Samuel. Don't miss verse 7: "Now Samuel did not yet know the Lord: The word of the Lord had not yet been revealed to him." God had provided Samuel with a godly mentor who could guide him into hearing from the Lord. The next time God called Samuel, he was ready.

Sometimes we miss the burning within us because we don't know how to listen to God's voice. As believers, God speaks into our lives all the time. He creates a flame within us to guide and direct us where He wants us to go, but we must know how to recognize that voice. God will provide us with mentors who will help us along the way, just like He did for Samuel. Seek those people in your Christian family who you know are mature in their faith and can help you discern God's voice. Tell them when you think you hear God's call and explain what you think you are hearing. Being able to share with and find guidance from a godly mentor is the best encouragement.

We Don't Want to Hear It

Realize, though, that sometimes we miss God's voice not because we don't understand but because we don't want to hear it. We hear something that doesn't align with our way of thinking, and we're reluctant to change. We often forget that this life is not all there is, and we lose our kingdom focus. We are so fixated on the here and now, the physical needs we have, that we forget about the spiritual needs that mean so much more. This happened to the Israelites. Jeremiah warned them of this repeatedly. Here are just a few examples:

- Jeremiah 6:10 – Their ears were closed, and they could not listen.

- Jeremiah 13:11 – Although the Israelites were God's chosen people, created to be close to God, they did not listen to Him.

- Jeremiah 17:23 – They did not incline their ears toward God; they were stiff-necked.

- Jeremiah 25:4 – The Lord sent prophets to speak the word of God to them, but they did not listen.

- Jeremiah 35:14 – He spoke to them repeatedly, but they would not listen.

These are just a few examples of what God told Jeremiah to say to the Israelites. God wanted His people to hear Him and heed His voice, but they wanted to go their own way. We are often prone to do the same. Somehow, we think we have a good plan for resolving whatever problem is in front of us. After deciding how to proceed, we ask for the Lord's blessing. That's backward. We must go to the Lord first, wait for His answer, and follow Him. That requires being in tune with His

Spirit and His voice. Don't ignore the burning within you. Incline your ear to the Lord, and you will hear Him.

We Wallow in Our Grief

Finally, like the men on the road to Emmaus, we can miss God's voice because of our downcast faces. In our deepest sorrow, sharpest disappointments, or moments of confusion, we keep our faces downcast. God says to do just the opposite. He says to lift up your head. Let's examine Psalm 24 to see how God wants to speak into your most challenging times.

First, in verses 1 and 2, realize who God is. He is the Maker of heaven and earth, and He owns it all, including you and me. It is God who holds everything together. Next, look at who can stand before God—those with clean hands and pure hearts. He wants our total devotion, with nothing getting in the way of our relationship with Him. In verses 7-10, God wants us to lift up our heads. Why? So, the King of Glory may come in. What an amazing God we serve! He wants to enter our lives; He wants to speak to us; He wants our heads lifted up, not downcast.

Jesus tried to help the men on the road to Emmaus understand all that had happened in Jerusalem and how He had fulfilled Scripture and overcome death. But they were so caught up in their grief, their faces were so downcast, they didn't recognize the burning within them. We too at times have this burning conviction within us. Jesus is trying to teach us something through a hardship that is difficult to understand. In those times, we need to hear Him say, "Lift up your head." Get your focus back onto Him. Don't ignore the burning within you.

Our Eyes Are Opened

Let's not forget why the men on the road to Emmaus said what they did in the following passage: "They asked each other, 'Were not our hearts burning within us while he talked with us on the road and opened the Scriptures to us?'" This question came after Jesus had revealed Himself to them. Their eyes had been opened. Looking back, the dusty road filled with potholes had become more apparent. They could remember their experience in Jerusalem not with downcast faces and sorrow but with a new understanding of the triumph amid the pain. God had a more desirable plan! They realized they should have known all along. They enjoyed great success now that they could see!

We too have this victory. We will suffer hardship. Sometimes our vision will be blurred, and discouragement may overwhelm us. However, Jesus will step in and teach us during those times, even if we don't recognize Him immediately. He will place that same burning within our hearts that He put in the men on the road to Emmaus. A spark inside us will convict us of opening our eyes to see Him. When we finally recognize His presence, we will have the same reaction: "Wasn't my heart burning within me?" Jesus was always there, beside us, teaching us. Our lives won't be the same when we come out on the other side. We will be able to look back and see the hand of God in all of it.

So don't ignore the burning within you. Fan the flame and see the victory the Lord brings to your life!

Journal Your Journey

Read Psalm 24 on the next page. Write about who God is, how powerful He is, and how this helps you lift up your head instead of keeping your face downcast.

Write a prayer of thanksgiving to the Lord for being the lifter of your head. Ask Him to step in to give you encouragement and joy.

Journey through the Book

1. What exactly is the "burning" within you that you experience when you read Scripture, hear a sermon, or any other way that God speaks?

2. What can cloud our vision and keep us from sensing the Holy Spirit?

3. What sometimes makes our hearts hardened toward hearing God speak?

Journey through Scripture

Meditate on the following passages to keep your focus on Jesus:
- Jeremiah 17:23
- 1 Samuel 3:10
- Psalm 24:3-4

Psalm 24

The earth is the Lord's and everything in it,
the world, and all who live in it;
for he founded it on the seas
and established it on the waters.
Who may ascend the mountain of the Lord ?
Who may stand in his holy place?
The one who has clean hands and a pure heart,
who does not trust in an idol
or swear by a false god.
They will receive blessing from the Lord
and vindication from God their Savior.
Such is the generation of those who seek him,
who seek your face, God of Jacob.
Lift up your heads, you gates;
be lifted up, you ancient doors,
that the King of glory may come in.
Who is this King of glory?
The Lord strong and mighty,
the Lord mighty in battle.
Lift up your heads, you gates;
lift them up, you ancient doors,
that the King of glory may come in.
Who is he, this King of glory?
The Lord Almighty—
he is the King of glory.

116

15

Share with Others

They got up and returned at once to Jerusalem. There they found the Eleven and those with them, assembled together and saying, "It is true! The Lord has risen and has appeared to Simon." Then the two told what had happened on the way, and how Jesus was recognized by them when he broke the bread (Luke 24:33-35).

After the men had this encounter with the risen Lord, they knew what they needed to do. They got up at once and returned to Jerusalem. No sitting around discussing it and trying to come to their own decision. No questioning if it was the right step to take. They simply got up and returned to Jerusalem to share what they had experienced.

Remember from the first chapter that this trip was about seven miles, a walk that would take about three hours at a leisurely pace. I think this return walk to Jerusalem was not at a relaxed pace, however. In their excitement, I'm sure they didn't waste any time returning so they could tell the others what they had experienced.

My Journey

I was excited but terrified when I finally realized God wanted me to share what He had done. This happened when

I was at worship team practice at my church. We always ended practice with prayer requests, prayer, and praises. My anniversary was coming up later that week, and I felt a burning in my spirit to give that as a praise. Immediately, the anxiety crept up on me. I thought, *As soon as I say that, they're going to ask how many years I've been married. I just can't say it.*

But then I found myself not just telling them my anniversary was coming up but explaining why I had never given that information as a praise in my life. I told them I had always just celebrated privately with my husband, so I didn't have to explain the math and bring up all that shame again. Before, it was never a praise for me but a private prayer request. I had spent six years wrestling with these thoughts and fears, and it was tough to open my mouth and speak it out loud. When I did, however, the words kept flowing.

And when I told my story, do you know what the rest of the worship team members did? They embraced me. They loved me. They told me everything God had tried to say to me for years. I didn't have to live in that shame. I savored one of the most liberating moments of my life. Instead of worrying about overhearing another conversation about me behind a wall, I had a group of people who understood that redemption comes from the Lord. When He forgives your sins, they are gone forever. I found a freedom I never had before—I could walk in His grace with my head held high, redeemed by the One who created me.

Encourage One Another

The Lord asks this of you as well. When the Lord works in your life, He wants you to share what He has done. Great encouragement comes when other believers share their testimony of redemption and victory, both for the ones telling the story and the ones listening. Others traveling a road of sadness can cling to these words of testimony and gain a glimpse of hope. The one giving the testimony receives a sense of love and acceptance from those listening and not passing judgment. Don't keep to yourself what God has done in your life. Get excited about it, share it with others, and let them celebrate with you. It is a risk. Some may judge, but it is a risk worth taking. Once you know who you are in Christ, the judgment of others no longer matters.

Let's break down the conversation when the two men found the disciples. They first said to them, "It is true!" If you look back to Luke 24:9-12, you'll see the disciples had been told about the empty tomb and the angel who had said He had risen from the dead. But they did not believe the women who told them this story. They thought it was nonsense.

They forgot God is the God of the impossible. Logically speaking, they knew that people don't rise from the dead. Even after all the miracles they had witnessed Jesus do, they still couldn't believe this devastation could be turned around. Remember that they had seen all the same horrifying events that the men on the road to Emmaus had witnessed. They were still in the place the two men were before their encounter with Jesus. They were still stuck in the pothole of despair and clouded vision. So, the first thing these two men told them was, "It is true!"

We have this same ability encourage others when God works in our lives. Try saying aloud, "God promised this in His Word, and it is true! Let me tell you what He's done for me." If we follow this with our testimony, we can give glorious hope to someone else who hasn't yet experienced a win themselves.

This is one more reason to not neglect meeting together. You never know the testimony you might hear from someone else that will touch your heart and give you the encouragement to keep trusting God. You never know when you will have the opportunity to share your personal victory with someone and provide them with the motivation they need to hear. Sometimes all we need to hear is, "It is true!" Sometimes, all someone needs is a gentle nudge from your willingness to share so others will look for God themselves.

Tell What Jesus Has Done for You

After the men told them that it was true that Jesus rose from the dead, they continued to talk about what had happened along the road to Emmaus. They didn't stop at "It is true" but shared the details of how Jesus revealed Himself to them. Words such as "God always keeps His promises" or "I know God has a plan and a purpose for everything" are good and proper. But sometimes, people need to hear more. Rather than just hearing that the promises are true, they need evidence to show them. When people struggle, a detailed story of victory and redemption from someone else can be just what they need to lift their heads.

Isaiah 52:7 says it this way: "How beautiful on the mountains are the feet of those who bring good news, who proclaim peace, who bring good tidings, who proclaim salvation, who say to Zion, 'Your God reigns!'" Be those beautiful feet to someone else; proclaim what God has done in your life. Don't just repeat the promises from Scripture, as beautiful and accurate as they are. Tell your story. Give others honest details of how God has tangibly fulfilled those promises in your life.

You Will Be His Witness

Our testimonies are an encouragement to others, and God also expects us to share it. Right before Jesus ascended into heaven, He said to His disciples, "You will be my witnesses in Jerusalem, and in all Judea and Samaria, and to the ends of the earth" (Acts 1:8). Yes, this was spoken to the disciples, but it applies to us today. We are to be witnesses for Jesus, telling people about Him every chance we get. Ephesians 5:16 and 1 Peter 3:15 speak to this, telling us to "make the most of every opportunity" and "always be prepared to give an answer to everyone who asks you to give the reason for the hope that you have."

We are to share our testimonies and speak about God's movement in our lives. God expects it. Jesus didn't say, "You might be my witnesses," or "Go and tell others what I have done when you feel like it or when you're not afraid." No, He said, "You will be my witnesses" (Acts 1:8). He expects that of us.

The Purpose for the Pain

This is the end goal of any kind of trial you go through. God is always trying to teach you something. You may have times of discouragement, sorrow, pain, and confusion, and sometimes, you may not be able to recognize Jesus. But He is always by your side. Jesus will never leave or forsake you. When you get through the trial and realize how Jesus was working all along, you can look back and appreciate the little ways He guided you, even when you didn't know it. Then you can go and tell others what He has done.

Our trials are often for that very purpose so that you can

encourage someone else who is going through something similar. Second Corinthians 1:3-4 says,

> *Praise be to the God and Father of our Lord Jesus Christ, the Father of compassion and the God of all comfort, who comforts us in all our troubles, so that we can comfort those in any trouble with the comfort we ourselves receive from God.*

So be His witness; tell others of all He has done for you!

This was the point of the dusty road all along. Jesus allowed you to walk on it and learn from Him so that you could help others in their difficulty. Remember, we were created for fellowship, for sharing with each other. We were never meant to walk this life alone. Every experience we have, good or bad, is to be shared with others to help and encourage them along the way. So, like these two men, get excited about what the Lord has done, and don't hesitate to tell others about it!

JOURNAL YOUR JOURNEY

Acts 1:8 says, "But you will receive power when the Holy Spirit comes on you; and you will be my witnesses in Jerusalem, and in all Judea and Samaria, and to the ends of the earth." Write about how you need to be a more effective witness for Christ. Choose one or two ways God has worked in your life that you could share with someone in the coming week. Then commit to doing that regularly.

Write a prayer asking God to give you the boldness you need to tell others about how He has worked in your life. Ask Him to bring people who need to hear your testimony into your life.

JOURNEY THROUGH THE BOOK

1. What blessings come from sharing your testimony with other believers? Think of the blessings received by both you and the people with whom you are sharing.

2. Remember that one of the main reasons for sharing your victories is to provide encouragement to others. What do you have to share that might encourage someone today?

3. Why do you think God expects us to share our testimonies and not just thank Him without sharing?

JOURNEY THROUGH SCRIPTURE

Meditate on the following passages to keep your focus on Jesus:
- Isaiah 52:7
- Acts 1:8
- Ephesians 5:16

CONCLUSION

I am honored and thankful that you chose to walk this road with me. Reading my story of struggle and redemption has hopefully encouraged your heart. I pray you have found redemption in your story along the way and that you can see Jesus clearer in your life. Most of all, even if you are in the middle of a struggle, I pray you can discern He is there. Remember that He loves you so much that He will never leave your side.

Know that you will probably walk down a road like this again. Hold on to some key ideas so that you can remain strong in the Lord when that time comes. First, remember the importance of having other Christians to talk to along the way. Find one or two people you trust so that you can go to them for advice and direction. Be sure to tell your story and give encouragement to other believers. You can always ask God questions such as, "Don't you get it?" and "Why isn't this turning out the way I thought it would?" Jesus will walk you through those times, not condemn you for feeling confused, afraid, or discouraged.

Most importantly, rely on God's Word for truth and invite Jesus into your daily life to provide you with your daily bread. Satan is good at lying, and he will try to deceive you into believing something totally contrary to what God says. You must be in the Word often if you are going to recognize these lies. You need to know the character and person of God so that you know when there is a voice speaking to you that is not His. And the best way to understand and live the Word is to have Jesus residing with you, guiding you. Jesus is your daily bread. He is the Bread of Life, the One who will sustain you through anything life throws your way. Don't let Satan tell you otherwise.

I don't know where you stand with the Lord right now. I know that His salvation and redemption are for everyone to experience. He died on the cross and rose from the dead so that nobody would have to live under condemnation and judgment. His sacrifice was for our eternal redemption and a beautiful redemption in our lives right now.

When Jesus steps into a situation, no condemnation or fear is there. He wants to be the Lord of your life, to walk beside you and carry you through all your difficulties. Jesus desires nothing more than for you to give your life to Him, submit to His will, and allow Him to guide you. He wants to take and throw away your pain, sorrow, and confusion and give you a glorious future of redemption.

If you have never taken that step of asking Him into your life, I pray that you would do that now. It is as simple as confessing your sins to Him and asking Him to come into your life to take the sin and shame away. Then, once you have asked Him into your life, put Him in His rightful place—on His throne as Lord. Rely on Him to determine your steps and future. Ask Him to give you His daily bread, to walk beside you, and take control of the present and the future. Just as He was with the men on the road to Emmaus, He will be with you. He will never leave your side.

If you have already taken the step of asking Jesus to be Lord of your life, look for places where you are not living in victory as you should. John 10:10 says, "I have come that they may have life, and have it to the full." He desires for you to have a fulfilled life in Him. We often believe in Jesus and His salvation, but we forget that He is so much more. If we are found in Him, we should have a contented and satisfying life because we have the only sustenance we need. Times of struggle, grief, confusion, or pain will come, but Jesus has overcome all that. He doesn't want us living in those places. He wants to set us free and live an abundant life in Him.

I have learned so much about myself by walking down this road to Emmaus with these two men, and I hope you have as well. I now understand better what it means to rely on His goodness to see me through. I realize that it is okay to walk through grief and that questioning does not show a lack of faith. Instead, it shows how much Jesus loves me and is willing to allow me to process that pain. I have a new appreciation of the love of Christ and a deeper knowledge of just how that love plays out in real life. I pray that along this journey, you have learned these things too. My heart's prayer for you, which I have already prayed over anyone who has found this book in their hands, is that of Ephesians 3:14-21:

> *For this reason, I kneel before the Father, from whom every family in heaven and on earth derives its name. I pray that out of his glorious riches he may strengthen you with power through his Spirit in your inner being, so that Christ may dwell in your hearts through faith. And I pray that you, being rooted and established in love, may have power, together with all the Lord's holy people, to grasp how wide and long and high and deep is the love of Christ, and to know this love that surpasses knowledge that you may be filled to the measure of all the fullness of God. Now to him who is able to do immeasurably more than all we ask or imagine, according to his power that is at work within us, to him be glory in the church and in Christ Jesus throughout all generations, for ever and ever! Amen.*

Author's Note

Suppose you already know Christ as your Lord and Savior. In that case, I pray that each chapter you have read in this book will draw you closer to Him and help you to recognize His presence more in your everyday life. I pray that the Scriptures given throughout this book have encouraged your faith and will become personal to you. I pray that when you walk through periods of loss, pain, or discouragement, this book will find you and help you understand how closely your Savior walks with you. And I pray that you have been able to see Jesus clearly and find His mighty redemption of your struggle at the end of it all.

If you are reading this and you do not know Christ, or are skeptical about Him, I pray that it has encouraged your heart. I hope you have read through the chapters with an open mind and looked up the Scriptures. I pray that God has spoken to your heart and that your eyes have been opened, just like the men when they sat down to eat with Jesus. I pray that you will see that you can live an eternity with this Lord who loves you so much. If you are in a time of struggle, I pray you have found hope and peace on these pages. There is no better walk than the one we can experience with the Lord.

Whatever your reason for reading this book, more than anything else, I pray that Jesus has been glorified by the words on these pages. Since recognizing Jesus on my road to Emmaus, my life has changed. Like the two men in Luke 24, I couldn't help but share this journey and experience with others. I want everyone to see that the Bible is truth, Jesus is alive and active in our lives, and we can know Him personally. Through the accounts of these men, other people in Scripture, and my story, I want people to see that redemption is possible. Life is beautiful when it is lived for Christ.

ABOUT THE AUTHOR

BRENDA TROUTMAN is a Bible-believing Christian who desires to share with others what she has learned from Jesus in her own life. Brenda has been married to her wonderful husband, Chris for twenty-two years, and the two of them have three children together. In her free time, Brenda enjoys reading, crocheting, walking, and enjoying nature. She resides in Punxsutawney, Pennsylvania, the town that she has called home for her entire life. Brenda is a member of the Punxsutawney Christian and Missionary Alliance, where she serves on the worship team and teaches Sunday school. She has also worked in Christian education for twenty years, serving as a Bible, math, and science teacher.

For book orders or to book speaking engagements, Brenda can be reached in the following ways:
• Email Brenda at brendatroutman86@gmail.com
• Send a message via Facebook at facebook.com/ ouremmausjourney
• Visit Brenda's website at ouremmausjourney.com and click on the "Connect with Brenda" tab

She would love to connect with you and pray with you as you walk down your road to Emmaus. She welcomes you to check out her website at www.ouremmausjourney.com and join her community on Facebook at facebook.com/ouremmausjourney. Come share your story of struggle and triumph and allow her to pray for you!

www.ingramcontent.com/pod-product-compliance
Lightning Source LLC
Chambersburg PA
CBHW071156120626
46546CB00006B/2288

* 9 7 8 1 9 5 6 3 6 5 3 3 7 *